Christmas Art &

Rhona Whiteford & Jim Fitzsimmons

Bright Ideas
for Early Years

Published by Scholastic Publications Ltd,
Villiers House, Clarendon Avenue,
Leamington Spa, Warwickshire CV32 5PR

© 1992 Scholastic Publications Ltd

Written by Rhona Whiteford and
Jim Fitzsimmons
Edited by Magdalena Hernas
Designed by Micky Pledge
Illustrations by Pat Murray
Photographs by Mike Turner (p. 5), Garry
Clarke (pp. 9, 17, 27, 35, 43, 53, 63, 73),
Chris Kelly (p. 79).
Cover design by Sue Limb
Cover photograph by Martyn Chillmaid

Artwork by Salvo Design and Print,
Leamington Spa
Typeset by Typesetters (Birmingham) Ltd
Printed in Great Britain by
Loxley Brothers Ltd, Sheffield

The publishers wish to thank the children and staff of Garswood Playgroup (Lancashire) and Catherine Infant School (Leicester) for their help in the preparation of this book.

British Library Cataloguing in Publication Data
A catalogue record for this book is available from the British Library.

ISBN 0 590 53041-0

All rights reserved. This book is sold subject to the condition that it shall not, by way of trade or otherwise, be lent, hired out or otherwise circulated without the publisher's prior consent in any form of binding or cover other than that in which it is published and without a similar condition, including this condition, being imposed upon the subsequent purchaser.

No part of this publication may be reproduced, stored in a retrieval system, or transmitted, in any form or by any means, electronic, mechanical, photocopying, recording or otherwise, without the prior permission of the publisher, except where photocopying for educational purposes within a school or other educational establishment is expressly permitted in the text.

Contents

Introduction 5

Room decorations 9

    A big bauble   10
    Snowflake hangings   10
    Stripy shapes   11
    Glitter-and-seed mobiles   11
    A chimney-pot post-box   12
    A wall frieze   12
    Window decorations   13
    Decorated fir trees   14
    A candle hanger   14
    Dribbled Christmas stockings   15
    Stained-glass windows   16

Tree decorations 17

    Fairy folk   18
    A Christmas rose   18
    Pasta garlands   19
    Fairies for the tree-top   20
    A tree cracker   21
    A candle on each branch   22
    Doves of peace   23
    Snow fans   23
    An oak-leaf decoration   24
    Spaghetti stars   24
    A painted pine-cone   25
    Pasta baubles   26

Table decorations 27

    A Christmas tree   28
    A pine-cone Christmas tree   28
    Table Christmas tree   29
    A candle table centre   29
    A Christmas cracker place-mat   30
    A Christmas cracker napkin ring   30

A party place-name 31
A party hat cutlery holder 31
A candle holder 32
Marbled candles 32
Christmas lanterns 33
Clay holly leaves 34

Christmas cards 35

A jewelled tree 36
A glitter drawing 36
A print of Rudolph 36
The three kings 37
A starry night 37
A pasta card 38
A bauble card 38
A green greeting 38
A fern tree 39
A sequin tree card 39
A snowstorm card 40
When Santa got stuck up the chimney 40
Glitzy wrapping-paper 41
Dazzlingly bright wrapping-paper 41
Marbled wrapping-paper 42

Calendars 43

A family bus trip 44
Our house 44
A self-portrait in a gilt frame 45
A calendar man 46
A monoprint masterpiece 46
An everlasting calendar 48
A paper sculpture calendar 49
A collage calendar 50
An antique metal plaque 50
A stained-glass window 51
Bouncing bits 52

Presents 53

A snowstorm 54
A pomander 54
A jewelled paperweight 55
A bookmark 56
A desk tidy 56
A decorated notebook 57
A vase of dried flowers 58
A decorated box 58
A dog-lead holder 58
Bookends 59
Pasta necklaces 60
A Christmas pudding tea-cosy and egg-cosies 60
A wall hanging 61
A key tidy 62
A coin paperweight 62

Hats, masks and costumes 63

A golden halo 64
A starshine circlet 64
A robin in the evergreens 65
A royal crown 66
The evening star 66
Animals and birds 67
A party-time mask 67
A second face 68
Variations on the face hat 68
Simple hats 69
A knight of the realm 70
Crêpe skirts and cloaks 70
Decorating fabric 72

Pictures 73

A winter evening 74
A stocking full of wishes 74

A Nativity scene (wax and wash)   75
A thumb-print picture   76
Three fancy kings   76
A 3-D snow scene   77
A frottage picture   78
A Christmas painting   78

Cookery   79

Chocolate medals   80
Fondant sweets   80
Pepparkakor biscuits   81
Marzipan sweets   82
Party dips   82
Chocolate truffles   83
Butterscotch fudge   84
Holly leaf biscuits   84
A Christmas log   85
St Nicholas' letter biscuits   86
Mincemeat   87
Chocolate apples   88

Puppets and scenery   89

A walking snowman   90
Waving puppets   90
The Nativity with straw puppets   91
The Nativity set   91
A puppet theatre   92
Felt finger puppets   92
Push-along puppets   93
Scenery   94
   Trees, bushes and walls   94
   Backdrops and buildings   94

Index   96

Introduction

Christmas time offers a wealth of opportunities for exciting work across the curriculum for all age groups. For those in the early years, however, art and craft is a particularly apt starting point, being the main anchor point for much of the curriculum at any time.

As early years teachers and carers know, this end of the educational spectrum requires much dedication, knowledge, energy and understanding as the child moves from a secure home base out into the wider world of school. It can be said that the three-to-six age group spans the greatest developmental range and, as a result, its teachers need a vast range of teaching strategies, opportunities and ideas to pour into the ever-ready minds of their charges.

Art and craft can open up education for pupils and teachers alike. It can provide opportunity for exploration of the environment and its materials, a chance for interaction with peers, a reason to learn and develop skills and techniques and a chance to make personal choices. It is a hands-on experience; it is fun; and you get something of your very own at the end – a model, a painting or a sense of achievement to fire greater endeavour.

Art and craft can help the early years child to develop hand control, spatial awareness, awareness of design, movement and forces, powers of observation and the vital skill of concentration.

At Christmas, when senses and hopes are high, what better time to provide art and craft opportunities and combine the excitement with enjoyable learning?

How to use this book

All the activities in this book require a greater or lesser degree of adult supervision. Many of the children may not have acquired the skills necessary for a particular task. When this is the case, the role of the adult is to teach the skills or techniques required. It may be that a child can only attempt two or three of the techniques involved in a particular task and that adult preparation or finishing off is necessary to complete it.

What is important here is that children should practise or learn a single skill and have an end product of which they feel proud. The youngest or most inexperienced in this age group will be able to do very little on their own as they struggle to master such giants as the wayward glue spreader. However, if all a child actually accomplishes is sticking several bits of tissue on the base paper, that is good enough as even in this short session a good teacher has an opportunity to help develop the child's powers of observation and discussion, visual perception of the work and possibly imagination too.

We preferred not to designate activities in this book to particular age groups, leaving it to the teacher to determine which of the skills the children can attempt. Obviously some of the tasks will require greater concentration spans and involve several processes and these will be most suitable for the more experienced children. However, it is possible to organise the work so that even the youngest can tackle a long task if the job is broken up into several sessions over a week.

Examine carefully the skills involved in a task and help the children with skills, even apparently easy ones such as the manipulation of glue spreaders,

paintbrushes and scissors – correct hand holds are very important and a little assistance can help a child to achieve success.

Do try a variety of tasks so that the children gain experience of many materials and techniques. Talk about the ongoing task to help the children conceptualise their experiences.

We can't stress enough the value of praise in the learning process. All children need this vital boost to develop confidence and to become creative in their own right.

Safety aspects

For most types of art and craft work, children in this age group will have an adult present to guide them and to discuss the work in progress. However, it is always wise to be vigilant where safety is concerned. Do remember to store all dangerous substances and equipment well out of reach of the children. These items include some adhesives, spray-paint cans, craft knives, pointed scissors and very small craft materials such as lentils, peas, seeds, sequins and buttons. Every teacher knows that even six-year-olds can inadvertently swallow or push such small items in ears, noses and eyes. Use any spray-paint in a well-ventilated area and keep the children out of the range of the spray, although you might let them have a go if you guide their hands.

Encourage safety awareness in the children and any classroom helpers, for example by getting them to spot dangerous items you have left unattended or to carry equipment such as scissors in a safe manner. Remind the children not to put small objects in their mouths or poke friends with sharp craft materials. Even art straws can cause damage if poked in an eye or down an ear and adhesives, paints and sand on a hard floor can cause someone to slip. Young children readily absorb safety advice in their 'code of rules' and can be quite helpful in maintaining safety standards.

Room decorations

Chapter one

When decorating a room at Christmas, the key association seems to be colour; and the colours we all recognise as festive are red, green, white, silver and gold. There is no need to strip the classroom of the existing decorations to create a Christmas atmosphere. Instead, you can add to existing displays by filling in a corner, edging a shelf or surrounding a door or window with perhaps one Christmas picture as a feature. (See *Bright Ideas Display* by Rhona Whiteford and Jim Fitzsimmons, Scholastic Publications, 1991 for some more ideas.) The ideas offered in this section include hangings, edgings, window coverings and the all-important Christmas post-box. Some items such as the snowflake hangings can be left on display after Christmas to form part of a general winter display.

A big bauble

What you need

Circles of white paper 25cm in diameter, small circles of tissue paper in assorted colours, PVA adhesive, glue spreaders, glitter, parcel ribbon.

What to do

Smear a small blob of the adhesive on the white circle. Stick the circles of tissue on the white circle, overlapping different colours.

Now load the glue spreader with adhesive and dribble it over the design in a circular motion until the adhesive has run out. Sprinkle the circle with glitter and leave to dry.

A bow and loop of parcel ribbon can be stapled to the top to complete the bauble.

Snowflake hangings

What you need

White cartridge paper, white crêpe paper or silver ribbon, silver foil, adhesive, a stapler, scissors.

What to do

Cut a circle of white cartridge paper to the size you want your snowflake to be and fold it into quarters. Cut out triangular shapes from each of the folded sides and a deep triangle from the open end.

Open up the snowflake and spread it out flat. Cut a circle of foil at least 3cm larger than the snowflake and stick the snowflake on it. Cut a strip of white crêpe paper about 5cm wide, or a length of silver ribbon, and either glue or staple the

snowflakes on to it. Make strips of different lengths by attaching more or fewer snowflakes to each strip. These can then be hung from the ceiling in large clusters.

Similar mobiles can be made using cut-out pictures from Christmas cards edged with glitter and stuck on to a circle of foil. These can be attached to a length of wide florist's ribbon and suspended from the ceiling.

What to do

Cut the foil into strips along the leading edge of the paper. Take a rectangle of activity paper 25cm × 15cm, cover it with adhesive and stick different-coloured strips of foil diagonally across it.

Ensure there are no spaces between the foil for the sugar paper to show and that the foil is well stuck down. Place a template on the foil-covered rectangle and draw around the shape. Cut it out. Use as part of a border around pin boards or hang from the ceiling by a 3cm-wide strip of crêpe paper.

Glitter-and-seed mobiles

What you need

Dried peas, sycamore keys, pressed leaves, dried honesty seed cases, gold or silver spray-paint, gold and silver sequins, glitter, adhesive, white card, crêpe paper or florist's ribbon, coloured foil.

What to do

Cut out a circle of white card 20cm in diameter and a circle of foil 24cm in diameter. Spread adhesive on the card circle and stick a selection of seeds in a regular pattern on to it. When dry, spray it gold or silver. Make sure the room is well ventilated or go outside to spray. (An adult should do this.) Leave it to dry, then stick it on to the circle of foil. Glue large gold or silver sequins all around the edge of the card circle and dab spots of adhesive in the spaces between the seeds. Sprinkle with glitter for extra sparkle. Use these as a border around pin boards or hang them as mobiles by attaching them to a length of florist's ribbon or to a strip of crêpe paper.

Stripy shapes

What you need

Foil in assorted colours, adhesive, sugar paper in assorted colours, crêpe paper, scissors, templates of a star, a cracker and a bell to fit within a 25cm × 15cm rectangle.

A chimney-pot post-box

What you need

A large cardboard box with a lid, a large sheet of black sugar paper, card, a large rectangular car sponge, white and black poster paint, painbrushes, cotton wool, scissors, adhesive.

What to do

Take the cardboard box and paint it black inside and out, including the lid. Leave it to dry. Cut a hole in the lid and make a cylinder out of black sugar paper for the chimney-pot. Fit this inside the hole and make sure that the cylinder is large enough to take standard Christmas card-sized envelopes.

Make some grey paint by adding white paint to the black and print brick shapes, using the car sponge, on to the main part of the chimney stack until it is covered. Leave to dry, then trim around the chimney top with cotton wool to represent snow.

The children can post their Christmas cards and letters to Father Christmas down the chimney-pot. The lid can be removed later to take out the cards.

A wall frieze

What you need

Rectangles of coloured foil (red, green, gold and blue), PVA adhesive, silver glitter, non-biological white soap powder, stencils of Christmas shapes (bell, tree, star and cracker), newspaper.

What to do

Cut a rectangle of coloured foil 30cm × 20cm. Choose a stencil of one of the Christmas shapes. Put the stencil on top of the coloured foil and apply the adhesive inside the stencil. Place the foil on another sheet of newspaper. Mix the soap powder with the glitter and sprinkle the mixture over the stencil. Cover it well, then gently shake off any excess on to the newspaper so that it can be used again. Remove the stencil shape carefully and leave it to dry before using it again.

Use the other stencils to make different shapes on different-coloured foil backgrounds. You can group the shapes together as a frieze running all the way along a wall or all around the room.

Window decorations

What you need

Acetate sheets in assorted colours, glitter in assorted colours, scissors, rubber-based adhesive, a stapler, Blu-tack.

What to do

To make six-pointed stars, cut out equilateral triangles in gold acetate film. Staple pairs of triangles together. Make an assortment of different sizes. Dab adhesive round the edges of the star and over the staple in the centre and cover liberally with glitter. When the stars are dry attach them to the window with Blu-Tack or, if condensation is a problem, fix them to the frame in the corners of windows.

Cut out holly leaves in green acetate film, berries in red, bells in gold, red or blue and decorate the edges with glitter and display as above.

Decorated fir trees

What you need

Three shades of ready-mixed green powder paint, brown paint, small sponges, large white, green or grey sugar paper, a brush, foil circles in assorted colours (5cm in diameter), a foil star, adhesive, glitter.

What to do

These trees are made with hand prints. To apply the paint to the hands, dip the sponges in the paint, squeeze gently and coat the hand well. Start by making a row of hand prints at the edge of the paper farthest away from you to form the bottom of the tree. Make the next rows shorter each time to form a ragged triangle shape. Make the prints along the edge of the triangle splay out to give the impression of fir branches.

Add a trunk with the brush and when dry, cut the tree out and mount it as part of a larger picture or on another piece of paper. Decorate the tree with circles of coloured foil and add a star at the top.

If the trees are to form part of a winter scene decorate them with glitter by painting the edges of the fingers of each row with adhesive and sprinkling them generously with glitter.

A candle hanger

What you need

White card, red and gold foil, powder paint in assorted colours, a pump-action sprayer filled with water, scissors, Copydex adhesive, washing-up liquid bottle, crêpe paper.

What to do

Cut out from card the shape of a candle the size you want the mobile to be. Put Copydex adhesive into the washing-up liquid bottle. Replace the nozzle so that a thin ribbon of adhesive comes out when it is turned upside down. Trickle or trail the adhesive in zigzags or waves across the body of the candle shape. Let the adhesive dry thoroughly.

Spray the candle shape with a fine mist of water from the sprayer. Do not wet the surface too much. Sprinkle different colours of powder paint over the whole candle. Leave it to dry and then carefully peel off the adhesive, which will leave a crisp white pattern in the paint. Mount the candle on a piece of coloured foil to

What to do

Make sure the children's clothes are well protected during this activity – aprons or overalls might be a good idea.

Cut the sugar paper into stocking shapes (see illustration). The stocking is decorated by dribbling glue over the paper in a random design and then adding colour by sprinkling powder paint on to the surface.

Put the adhesive into yoghurt pots and provide brushes or spreaders. Scoop up a good brush full, and, holding the brush over the paper, let the adhesive dribble down. As it does so, move the brush around to make the line 'walk' all over the paper. Paint the top of the stocking with adhesive in smooth strokes so that you can get a full cover of colour at the next stage.

Put the powder paint into shallow containers and sprinkle it all over the stocking using the fingers. You can use a single colour or several, but if you choose the latter, drop the powder in patches so that the colours do not mix together. If, however, you want to show how primary colours mix to make new colours, this is a good opportunity.

Now pick up the stocking and shake it gently to leave the paint sticking to the gluey lines, and a haze of colour on the rest of the paper. The top of the stocking should have a thick band of colour.

Notes

Cover the work surface with paper so that you can salvage the powder paint for further use. You can add glitter to the paint or you can use it instead of paint. Alternatively, do one lot of dribbling with paint and then do a second lot which you can cover with glitter to add textural variety.

Stick a ribbon of crêpe paper on the top corner of the stocking to hang it by.

match the powder paint used and add a flame made from red and gold foil at the top of the candle. Hang from the ceiling on a 3cm-wide strip of crêpe paper.

Dribbled Christmas stockings

What you need

White sugar paper, PVA adhesive, dry powder paints in assorted colours, gold glitter, crêpe paper, paintbrushes or glue spreaders, yoghurt pots, small shallow containers, scissors.

Stained-glass windows

What you need

Rectangles or squares of tissue paper in assorted colours, PVA adhesive, a sheet of clear polythene, glue spreaders.

What to do

Place the polythene sheet on a flat surface. Spread adhesive on the sheet and, starting in the centre, lay the tissue shapes on to it, using the lighter colours first. Overlap the shapes to create different tones and shades of colour. Use one colour at a time and blend it into the next one gradually, to create rings of colour spreading outwards.

As you move towards the edge of the polythene sheet, pick the darker colours. You may decide to concentrate on the warm colours of yellow, orange, pink, purple, red and brown – or, alternatively, the cool colours of white, pale blue, pale green, lilac and dark blue. Finally, cover the whole sheet with a coating of PVA adhesive which, when dry, will give a translucent sheen. The sheet can be hung in front of a window as it is or the dried applique can be peeled off and hung up.

Cellophane squares can be used to create a similar effect, but the colours are more intense. Overlapping cellophane shapes give a greater range of tones and shades of colour in the finished window.

Notes

The polythene 'stained-glass windows' can be any size, either small rectangles created by individual children for displaying side by side, or one large 'window' created by a group of children. The sheets can be mounted in a frame of black card or cut into Christmas shapes such as stars, crackers or bells.

Tree decorations

Chapter two

The Christmas tree is the central decoration in the festive season and it features at home, in the school hall and often in the classroom too. Making tree decorations is an important part of the fun of Christmas and each child could make a decoration to take home as a contribution to the family tree. And as part of the school community preparations, each class could make a set of decorations to adorn the school tree. If you are part of a very large establishment, each class could be allocated a different type of decoration. The decorations described in this chapter are very traditional and have a Victorian feel about them. All are cheap and relatively easy to make and produce beautiful results.

Fairy folk

What you need

White net, glitter, dolly pegs (push-on type), old Christmas cards, gold spray-paint, large sequin stars, Copydex adhesive, a glue spreader, scissors.

What to do

To make the fairy's wings, cut a piece of net about 16cm × 30cm. Using a Formica surface, spread adhesive along the two longest edges and then sprinkle with glitter. Allow to dry thoroughly.

Cut out a small figure of an angel, child or animal from the Christmas cards. You can add a couple of large sequins for decoration.

Spray the peg gold and when dry, add adhesive, then glitter, to the head, the back and the bottom half of the front. Now stick the cut-out figure to the bare space and leave to dry.

Gather up the net along its length and staple firmly at the gathered point. Add a touch of adhesive there and slide the wings between the forks of the peg to complete the fairy.

A Christmas rose

What you need

Double-sided foil, clothes-pegs (spring type), glitter, gold spray-paint, adhesive, scissors, a pencil.

What to do

Cut out 10cm circles in foil and snip all round the edge at about 1cm intervals, 2cm- to 3cm-deep cuts. Using a pencil, curl alternate segments inwards to show the reverse colour. To complete the flower, put a blob of adhesive and glitter in the centre.

Take a gold-sprayed peg, cover its sides and ends with adhesive and cover in glitter. The flower is then attached to the peg with adhesive and, when dry, can be clipped to the branches of the Christmas tree.

Pasta garlands

What you need

Gold spray-paint, pasta tubes and bows, strong thread, a long, blunt threading needle, gold glitter, adhesive, scissors.

What to do

Use 2m of thread, doubled and knotted at the end to thread alternate bows and tubes of pasta. Tie off the end with a knot and leave about 10cm to make a join later.

Spray this small garland with gold spray-paint on both sides, making sure this is done in a well-ventilated place (an adult should do this).

Dab a little adhesive on each piece of pasta or on one type of the shapes only and sprinkle with gold glitter. The tubes look attractive with a line of glitter along their length. The opposite side can also be glittered if you like.

Make as many garlands as you need to decorate the tree. Join them together by tying the threads to the knots and snipping off the ends.

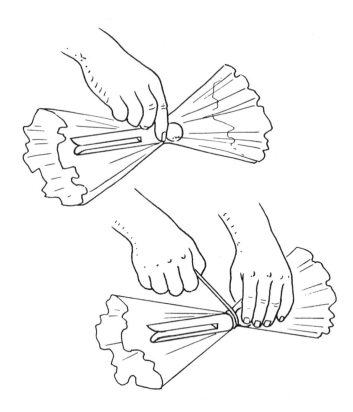
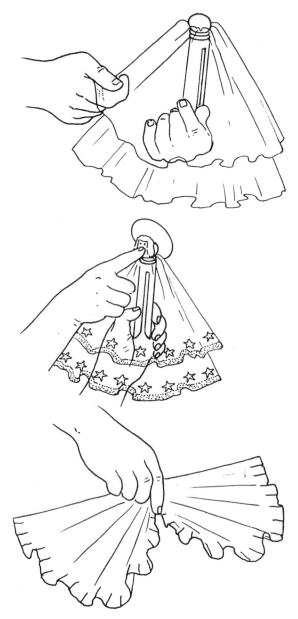

Fairies for the tree-top

What you need

Coloured acetate film, large sequins, glitter, dolly pegs (push-on type), old Christmas cards, double- or single-sided foil, pipe cleaners, scissors, adhesive, a stapler.

What to do

To make the fairy's skirt, cut a piece of acetate film about 25cm × 30cm and gather it round the neck of the peg (see illustration). This can then be fixed in place by twisting a pipe cleaner round it. Pull one side of the skirt over the pipe cleaner to make a double skirt and expose the head of the peg.

Paint the edges of the skirt with adhesive and sprinkle them with glitter. Stick some large sequins near the neck and on the skirt (star-shaped ones look very attractive).

To complete the head, cut a circle of gold foil for an angel or a large star for a fairy and glue these behind the head. For the face, cut out a large face from a Christmas card and glue it to the front. For added sparkle, put glitter on the rest of the peg head.

To make the wings, cut a semicircle of foil about 20cm in diameter and make cuts along the curved edge. These can be

slightly curled out to look like feathers. Carefully gather the centre back of the wings and, if necessary, secure with a staple. The wings can then be glued to the back of the neck and upper back of the figure. Gently curve the wings outwards and backwards. The figure can be pegged to the top of the tree or a branch of holly.

A tree cracker

What you need

Coloured acetate film, gold spray-paint, a clothes-peg (spring type), pipe cleaners, a narrow cardboard tube or a sweet container, glitter, a small motif (a foil shape or a dried flower), adhesive, scissors,

What to do

Cut the cardboard tube into lengths of about 6cm. Cut out 18cm squares from the acetate film. Roll each tube segment in the acetate film, twisting the ends and fixing them with a twist of pipe cleaner if needed. Tease out the open ends of the cracker to look full and rounded and stick on the motif.

To attach the cracker to the tree, make a clip, by spraying the peg with gold paint and then painting the sides and handle ends with adhesive. Dip in glitter. When dry, stick the cracker to the top of the peg along its length.

A candle on each branch

What you need

Egg-boxes, red paint, gold foil paper, gold or silver glitter, sequins, clothes-pegs (spring type), a thick crayon or dowel, orange acetate film, Copydex adhesive (most suitable because it dries very quickly and makes the process quicker), scissors.

What to do

Cut out the egg-holders from the boxes and paint them red. When dry, dip the top rim in the adhesive and then in glitter. Alternatively, you can stick sequins on the adhesive.

To make the candle, cut a piece of gold foil paper about 8cm × 10cm. Wrap it round a dowel or a thick crayon and glue the edge. Spread adhesive round the top of the candle and dip or roll it in glitter.

Make the flame by tearing a piece of orange acetate film and twisting the end, which you then dip in adhesive and push gently into the glittered end of the candle. Then glue the candle into its holder.

To make the clip, spray a clothes-peg with gold paint (spray several pegs at once to have some ready for other activities). Spread some adhesive over the clip sides and ends. These can then be covered with glitter or sequins.

Fix the candle holder to the top of the clip with adhesive and clip it to the end of a branch on the tree.

Doves of peace

What you need

Clothes-pegs (spring type), white card or thick glossy paper, large gold and silver sequins, adhesive, scissors.

What to do

Make a stencil of the bird shape. The children who are able can draw round and cut out their own birds. Glue round the edges or part of the outline and stick on alternate gold and silver sequins. Allow to dry.

Make a soft crease down the medial line of the bird from beak to tail and stick the flat edge of the clothes-peg to the underside at the head end of the bird. This can now be clipped to the tree, picture frames, flower arrangements, wreaths or stockings.

Snow fans

What you need

White A4 duplicating paper, silver glitter, thin silver ribbon, adhesive, a stapler.

What to do

Cut the A4-sized paper into three pieces across the width to give pieces 10cm by 21cm. Cut as many as you need. Fold them into small fans across the shortest side and staple the bottom.

Dab some adhesive along the open edge of the fan or dip it into a saucer of the adhesive. Now dip the sticky edge into a deep saucer full of glitter.

Make bows from the silver ribbon and attach them to the handle-end of the fans to complete the decoration.

An oak-leaf decoration

What you need
Card, dried oak leaves, gold spray-paint, assorted large sequins, parcel ribbon, PVA adhesive, scissors.

What to do
Cut a heart shape from a piece of strong card. Take three or four of the oak leaves and spray them gold (an adult should do this). Leave them to dry, then glue them in place on the piece of card. Decorate the leaves with large sequins. Dab some PVA adhesive on the leaves and sprinkle glitter over them. When completely dry, punch a hole at the top of the piece of card and thread a length of parcel ribbon through to hang on the tree. If you cannot use dried leaves, cut leaf shapes from coloured foil and use those instead.

Spaghetti stars

What you need
Card, lengths of spaghetti roughly the same size, gold or silver spray-paint, glitter, lentils, parcel ribbon, strong coloured foil, scissors, PVA adhesive.

What to do
Cut out a circle of card to the desired size and spread with adhesive. Stick on lengths of spaghetti so that they radiate out from the centre (see illustration).

A painted pine-cone

What you need

Pine-cones, strips of felt or ribbon, double-sided foil, red or white paint, glitter, scissors, adhesive.

What to do

Dip the pine-cone in paint and leave to dry. Apply dabs of adhesive to the edges and sprinkle glitter all over.

Cut out three holly leaves from the foil. (You may need to give the children ready-cut ones, or help them cut them out.) Stick the leaves to the base of the pine-cone (see illustration).

Turn the pine-cone upside down and glue a loop of ribbon or felt to the bottom.

Apply more adhesive to the centre and sprinkle it with lentils, enough to cover the spaghetti ends. Now spray the circle gold or silver (an adult should do this) and leave to dry. Next, brush the lentils with PVA adhesive and sprinkle with glitter. Cut a circle of coloured foil larger than the circle of card and glue the spaghetti star on to the circle of foil. Punch a hole in the top of the foil circle, thread a loop of parcel ribbon through the hole and hang the star on the tree.

Pasta baubles

What you need

Card, blue foil, pasta shapes, silver spray-paint, glitter, PVA adhesive, a paintbrush, scissors.

What to do

Cut out a circle of card about 6cm in diameter. Spread with the adhesive and decorate with pasta shapes. Spray with silver paint and leave to dry. Cut out a star or a bauble shape from the blue foil and stick the pasta-decorated circle on to it. Now brush the pasta shapes with a little PVA adhesive and sprinkle with glitter. If you have made two of the same shape, you can stick them back to back with a loop of ribbon in between so that the decoration can be hung on a branch of the tree.

Table decorations

Chapter three

This chapter provides ideas for large and small decorations, personal items as well as things for all to enjoy. You may want to make the individual place settings for the school party or for the children to take home. Similarly, small groups of children could make the Christmas trees for the party table. The Christmas lanterns which use a lighted candle are not suitable for a school party and can be made for use at home. However, they could be lit and placed out of reach of the children to brighten up a dark winter's afternoon in the classroom, perhaps at story-time to add sparkle to a Christmas tale.

A Christmas tree

What you need

Green sugar paper, coloured foil, crêpe paper in assorted colours, a large-size plastic cream pot, brown poster paint, PVA adhesive, scissors.

What to do

Take a sheet of green sugar paper and cut a semicircle to make a cone the size you want your tree to be. Make the cone tight so that it will stand on top of the cream pot. Mix brown poster paint with the adhesive (two parts adhesive to one part paint) and paint the cream pot. Leave it to dry. Apply adhesive round the bottom of the pot, turn it upside down and stick it inside the cone.

Decorate the tree by winding strips of fringed crêpe paper or folded concertina strips of green foil around the cone. Alternatively, the plain cone shape can be decorated with circles of coloured foil to represent baubles. Tinsel can also be added if desired. The top can be finished off with a gold foil star.

A pine-cone Christmas tree

What you need

Large pine-cone, dark green paint, gold or silver spray-paint, assorted sequins, thin- and medium-width parcel ribbon, a cotton reel, Blu-Tack, scissors.

What to do

Use the largest pine-cone you can find and make sure it is dry and open. Paint it dark green or spray it gold or silver. Remember to spray outside or make sure there is adequate ventilation (an adult should do this). Leave the cone to dry, then glue it on to the cotton reel. Decorate it with large sequins and a sequin star for the top. Thread lengths of thin parcel ribbon amid the 'branches' and tie a length of wider parcel ribbon around the cotton reel. If the pine-cone is top-heavy, it can be stabilised with a little Blu-Tack placed underneath the cotton reel.

to be, to make a template for the children to draw around. This will ensure that all the trees you make will be the same size. Place the template on the green sugar paper (or green card for larger trees) and draw round it. Cut out the tree shape and fold it vertically down the middle.

Use the collage materials, foil and glitter to decorate the front of the tree. Glue four of these back to back to make a free-standing tree for the party table.

A table centre

What you need

A plastic margarine tub, a ball of Play-Doh, cartridge paper, gold foil, orange and yellow tissue paper, florist's ribbon, shiny unbreakable baubles, holly and other available evergreens, poster paint, PVA adhesive, scissors.

What to do

Mix the poster paint with the PVA adhesive (two parts paint to one part adhesive) and paint the margarine tub. Leave it to dry. Make a tight tube of cartridge paper to represent the candle and stick a flame shape of orange and yellow tissue with a gold foil centre on top. Trickle adhesive down the candle and sprinkle with glitter. Take a lump of Play-Doh and make a hole in the centre to hold the candle. Press the Play-Doh on to the bottom of the inside of the margarine tub and fit the candle in place, making sure it does not wobble. Now take the evergreens and press them into the Play-Doh all around the bottom of the candle, so that they stick out over the edge of the tub. Make a bow of the florist's ribbon and stick it on to the candle. Place a couple of unbreakable shiny baubles at the base.

Table Christmas tree

What you need

Green card or sugar paper, shiny collage materials, card, glitter, foil, adhesive, scissors.

What to do

Draw the shape of a Christmas tree on a piece of card the size you want the tree

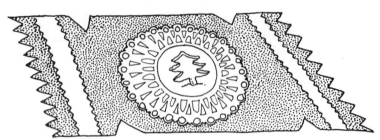

A Christmas cracker place-mat

What you need

A rectangle of coloured sugar paper 30cm × 22cm, gold or silver doilies, coloured foil, pictures cut out from old Christmas cards, pinking shears, scissors, adhesive.

What to do

Take the rectangle of sugar paper and fold it in half along the middle of the longest edge. Make a triangular cut on the top and bottom edge 5cm in from the open edges and cut triangles all the way down the open edges. Open up the paper and you will have a cracker shape.

Glue the Christmas-card cut-out in the centre of the paper doily and glue the doily in the centre of the cracker. Trim strips of coloured foil with pinking shears and decorate the cracker with the strips.

Christmas cracker place-names can be made in a similar way. Fold a square of card in half and cut out triangles in the top and bottom edges to make a cracker shape.

The edges can be coloured with felt-tipped pen if cutting through folded card is too difficult for the children.

The children can write their name on the card and then decorate it with sequins, glitter and a cut-out Christmas picture.

A Christmas cracker napkin ring

What you need

A cardboard tube, braid, sequin waste, a sequin strip, a paper napkin, paint, glitter, a Christmas-card cut-out, adhesive, scissors.

What to do

Paint or spray the cardboard tube and leave it to dry. Decorate with sequin waste by wrapping it around the middle. Edge this with braid and a sequin strip, and decorate with a cut-out Christmas-card picture. Place a napkin inside the tube and arrange it to look like the ends of a Christmas cracker.

What to do

Take the card and fold it to make a rectangle 20cm × 15cm. Stick the gummed paper circle to the front so that the top of the circle sticks up above the ridge of the folded card. Fold the top of the circle over the ridge. Draw in the eyes, nose and mouth.

Take a strip of gold card 10cm × 12cm and cut one edge in the shape of a crown. Attach the crown to the back of the folded card with the crown shape sticking up above the ridge.

Before the glue sets, turn the card around and make sure the crown is aligned with the face, then decorate it with sequins and glitter.

Add twisted wool for hair or draw it in with the felt-tipped pens. Use a glue pen to write the name and sprinkle glitter over it.

A party hat cutlery holder

What you need

Card, gold card, tin foil or crinkled foil, a Christmas-card cut-out or child's own picture, plastic cutlery, adhesive, scissors.

What to do

Cut a circle of gold card 15cm in diameter. Make a cylinder from a rectangle of card 10cm × 20cm. Cover the cylinder with crinkled foil or tin foil and glue it on to the circle of gold card. When the glue has dried, decorate the cylinder with the cut-out or the child's picture edged with glitter. Put in the plastic cutlery and a flag with the child's name on it. The holder can also double as a place-name for the party.

A party place-name

What you need

A rectangle of card 20cm × 30cm, glitter, sequins, gold or silver card, a circle of pink gummed paper, yellow, brown and black wool, scissors, felt-tipped pens, adhesive, a glue pen.

A candle holder

What you need

Self-hardening clay or play dough, clear varnish (in a spray) or gold spray-paint, dry seeds and pulses, a slim candle.

What to do

Take a piece of clay the size of a small apple and roll it into a ball. Hold it in the palm of your hand and press the candle end gently into the clay to a depth of about 3cm. Stand this on a board to flatten the base and so that you can decorate it. Using dried peas, sunflower seeds, pumpkin seeds, shells or any other small items, make a pattern round the candle and the sides. Press the items firmly into the clay but try not to wiggle them once in place so that the clay sets round them.

Leave the candle holder to dry thoroughly before going on to the next step. If you are using play dough, bake the candle holder for three hours at the lowest temperature and then use a quick-drying rubber-solution glue to fix the decorations. You may have to shave a little wax from the base of the candle to make it fit once the dough has been baked.

To finish off, remove the candle and spray the holder either with the clear varnish or with gold paint (an adult should do this). If you use gold paint, you can also sprinkle the candle holder with gold glitter while the paint is still wet for extra texture and light.

Play dough recipe
2 cups flour
1 cup water
1 cup salt
1 tbsp cooking oil

Knead all the ingredients together until they form pliable dough. Store in an airtight container.

Marbled candles

What you need

A white candle, emulsion or oil-based paints in bright colours and white, a bucket of cold water, a plastic cup, newspaper, scissors, a stick, string, white spirit.

What to do

This activity can be quite messy, so take care to spread plenty of newspaper and make sure the children wear aprons and rubber gloves. Throughout the activity, the children should be closely supervised.

Cut the top half of the plastic cup off and paint the bottom half with white emulsion paint. Leave it to dy. Fill the bucket with cold water and drop a blob of oil paint into it with a stick. If it does

not spread out add a little white spirit. Drop in some more colours and swirl the water around. Hold each candle by its wick and dip it into the bucket. Slowly lift it out and stand on newspaper to dry.

Make a hole in the bottom of the plastic cup and thead a piece of knotted string through the bottom. Dip the cup into the bucket and when the paint has dried stick the candle into the cup.

Christmas lanterns

What you need

A large glass jar, glitter, acetate film or tissue paper in assorted colours, paint, Plasticine, adhesive, small candle.

What to do

Cover the outside of the glass jar with shapes cut from acetate film or tissue. Dip the rim of the jar in adhesive and cover with glitter. Place a lump of Plasticine in the bottom of the jar and press in a candle. Make sure it is fixed firmly so that it does not fall over. When you light the candle, it will cast a flickering coloured light through the glass.

Other ways of decorating the jar include trailing different colours of paint down the outside, sticking on sequins and blobbing on fingerprints of colour.

Clay holly leaves

What you need

Clay (preferably a brand which needs no firing) or play dough (see recipe on page 32), acrylic paint or powder paint in dark green and red mixed with PVA adhesive, clear varnish (non-toxic), a holly leaf pastry cutter or a plastic lemonade bottle, brown or black pipe cleaners, a thick piece of cork tile, bark or wood to mount the ornament, rubber-based adhesive, a rolling pin, a ball-point pen.

What to do

Collect real holly leaves to observe before making the clay ones. Roll out the clay to about 1cm thickness and cut out three leaves. To make a holly leaf cutter, cut a large plastic drinks bottle into strips about 4cm wide. Now fold the strip in the centre backwards from the curve and make two more folds on each side of the central fold in the same way. Staple the edges together.

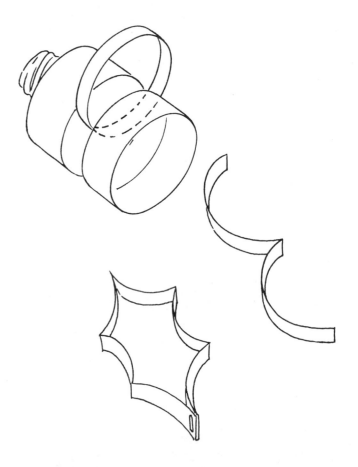

Draw veins on the leaves using an old ball-point pen and curve the leaves backwards from the central rib to imitate real ones. When they are dry (or when you have fired them), paint them dark green, letting the top side dry before going on to the bottom. The acrylic or the PVA adhesive both help to strengthen the clay. You can add a little silver glitter to the edges at this stage. The leaves can later be varnished to a high gloss. Make about five large red berries using the same method, but when they are first formed push a 10cm length of pipe cleaner into each one.

To mount the leaves, twist the berry stalks together to make a bunch and arrange it in the centre of the leaves on the cork, bark or wood mount. Use a good bed of adhesive to sit them on.

Christmas cards

Chapter four

The ideas for Christmas cards and wrapping paper featured in this chapter involve a variety of art techniques using paper, card, adhesives, paint and other media. Children are given an opportunity to practise skills such as cutting, printing, painting and collage with man-made and natural materials. And, although the designs for each card idea are already laid out, they can make their own choices within the offered framework.

Cards can be the size of a conventional greetings card or larger. When adding the greeting inside the card, write it on a separate piece of paper and stick it in when the card is complete to keep it neat and clean. Encourage the very best presentation: those who can write might like to add coloured decorations round the edge of the paper. Those who can't contribute to the greeting could add similar, simple decorations and an attempt at their own name.

A jewelled tree

What you need

Gold card or card covered in green foil, assorted sequins, a large sequin star, red foil, adhesive, scissors.

What to do

Fold the card in half and draw the shape of a fir tree in a tub with two of the tree branches touching the folded edge. Make this hinge generous.

Cover the tub front in red foil and cut out the tree shape, leaving the hinged branches intact. Paint a strip of adhesive across the curve of the branches and sprinkle liberally with sequins. Add a star at the top of the tree.

A glitter drawing

What you need

White card, white paper, coloured foil, glue pens, large glitter in another colour, scissors.

What to do

This is a card for those who can draw something (anything!), even if it is not yet recognisable in adult terms.

Use white card covered with coloured foil as the backing card. Cut out a rectangle of paper for the artist to draw on, then stick it on to the backing card.

Using a round-pointed glue pen, draw simple pictures such as a face, a tree or a house – a Christmas theme if possible, but a design of free lines or ordered lines is just as nice.

Sprinkle the glitter on with a salt shaker or by hand, then tap off the excess.

A print of Rudolph

What you need

Orangey brown, white and red paint in saucers, coloured foil, white card, grey paper, small twigs, cotton wool, sponge scraps, adhesive, black felt-tipped pen, scissors.

What to do

Cut and fold a conventionally shaped white card. Cut a rectangle of grey paper to fit the front, leaving a white border around. For Rudolph, use sponge scraps

The three kings

What you need

Black card, saucers of paint in assorted colours, triangles of sponge, three kings' heads cut out from old Christmas cards, a large gold foil star, glitter, scissors, adhesive.

What to do

Make a conventionally shaped greetings card from the black card and, using sponge triangles, carefully print three different-coloured triangles of paint on to it. Let them dry and stick a king's head on each. Add a wide strip of glitter to the bottom of each of the triangular robes, finishing the card off with a large star in the top right corner of the card.

A starry night

What you need

Black, white or blue foil card, Copydex adhesive, gold or silver glitter, yellow paint, a star-shaped pastry cutter.

What to do

Make a greetings card. Pour the adhesive into a saucer and dip the holding edge of the pastry cutter sparingly in the adhesive. Print carefully on the front of the card. Repeat until you have filled the space with glue prints. You can also try overlapping the prints. Sprinkle glitter liberally over the prints and tap off the excess. When the adhesive is properly dry dip your finger in the yellow paint and put a dot in the centre of each star to complete the card.

to print a large body and a head. Print the legs with the edge of the little finger, and the tail, ears and a red nose with the fingertips. Add snowflakes with fingertips and snow around Rudolph's feet with sponge. If you prefer, use cotton wool for snow.

Use two little twigs for Rudolph's antlers. To complete his face, draw eyes and a mouth with the felt-tipped pen when the paint has dried. For a splash of colour, add a coloured foil star to the sky and mount the picture on the front of the white card.

A pasta card

What you need

Dried pasta in a variety of shapes, stiff card, adhesive, gold spray-paint, gold or silver glitter, scissors.

What to do

Cut a piece of card twice the finished width and fold in half with a good crease. Let the children experiment with pasta shapes until they have a design they like. This could be a Christmas tree, a bauble shape, a star, a cracker. Lift up one pasta shape at a time from the original design, apply adhesive and replace in its position.

When the adhesive is thoroughly dry, spray the card and the pasta design with gold paint and sprinkle a little glitter on it before it dries (an adult should do this). Remember to use the spray in a well-ventilated place. You can also put the glitter on later, using adhesive.

A bauble card

What you need

Thin white card or stiff paper, coloured foil, sequins, glitter, braid, parcel ribbon, gold thread, a bauble template, scissors, adhesive.

What to do

Cut a piece of card twice the finished size and fold in half. Some children will be able to draw round the template and cut out their own baubles. Take three or four of the bauble shapes and decorate them with glitter, sequins and braid.

Stick two strips of ribbon down the sides of the card and add the baubles to the card, overlapping them slightly for a 3-D effect. Add lengths of gold thread for hangers to finish the card.

A green greeting

What you need

Gold foil, card covered in red or green foil, dried natural materials (honesty pods, oak leaves, beech leaves, alder cones, poppy heads), a cut-out picture of an animal from a greetings card, a cut-out greeting from a Christmas card, Copydex adhesive, scissors.

A fern tree

What you need

A pressed frond bracken fern, white card, red or green foil, glitter, white cartridge paper, a sequin star, adhesive, scissors.

What to do

Make a greetings card out of white card. Stick a rectangle of red foil on the front so that you have a 1cm-wide border all round. Now cut a piece of cartridge paper to fit inside this leaving wider borders at the sides.

Stick the fern frond carefully in the middle of the card, using tiny blobs of adhesive. To complete the card, add a small tub cut out from foil in a contrasting colour, a star and a tiny blob of glitter on the end of each arm of the 'tree'.

A sequin tree card

What you need

Sequin waste, assorted sequins, gold card or card covered in coloured foil, parcel ribbon, glitter, adhesive, scissors.

What to do

Cut a rectangular greetings card from the gold card or card covered in foil.

Cut a tall triangle from the sequin waste and apply a little glue round the edges only; then stick it centrally on the face of the card. Add a tub for the tree cut from a contrasting colour of foil.

Now dress the tree with coloured sequins for baubles and a star for the top. Tie a ribbon bow along the side to complete the card.

What to do

Make a folded greetings card from foil-covered card and stick a gold-foil oval shape on the front. When this is dry, let the children experiment with arranging a small selection of the dried materials, the animal picture and the greeting on the gold-foil shape. Try different arrangements, with the animal and the plants at the bottom and the greeting at the top, the greeting at the bottom and the leaves surrounding it and so on. When the artist is satisfied, the different items can be stuck down with small blobs of Copydex.

A snowstorm card

What you need

White card, silver glitter, green foil paper, a silver sequin star, large rectangular paper doilies, Copydex adhesive, scissors, paintbrush, black card.

What to do

Cut a rectangle of card and lay the doily over the card. Brush into the pattern with the adhesive. Lift the doily off very carefully and sprinkle the glitter liberally over the wet glue. Tap off the excess and leave to dry thoroughly.

Stick the foil to card and when dry cut out a fir tree. The children who are able can draw round a stencil and cut out their own tree. Stick the star to the top or cover the whole tree with coloured stars. The tree can now be mounted on the snowy background with a simple bracket which is made by folding a piece of card (8cm × 2cm) into an 'M' as shown. Glue one side to the tree back and allow to dry, then glue the other end to the front of the card. Use two of these, one at the top and one at the bottom to give a 3-D effect.

Mount this picture on a conventional folded shape made of black card.

When Santa got stuck up the chimney

What you need

Small rectangular pieces of sponge, brown and orange paint, white card, a picture of Santa cut from an old Christmas card, silver glitter, cotton wool, orange sugar paper, scissors, adhesive.

What to do

Cut a rectangle of orange paper for the chimney and print it with a brick pattern, using pieces of sponge and orange and brown paint. Let the children practise the interlocking tessellated pattern first.

Glitzy wrapping-paper

What you need

A large sheet of white paper or coloured, thin poster paper, gold and silver glitter, red and yellow paint, pastry cutters (hearts, circles, stars, fir trees), Copydex adhesive, salt cellars, scissors, a saucer.

What to do

Put the adhesive in the saucer and dip the holding edge of the pastry cutter in the adhesive. Copydex is not as viscous as the PVA so it is more suitable for printing. Print glue shapes all over the paper, touching the shape down carefully, perhaps taking two prints from each load of adhesive before dipping in again. You can choose an ordered pattern such as alternate rows of trees and stars or a random design. Take care not to smudge the prints before applying glitter.

Now shake the glitter from an old salt cellar or scatter it by hand all over the printed sheet. Roll the glitter from edge to edge to give a good coverage. To add a little colour to white paper, put a fingertip of red or yellow paint in the centre of some of the shapes.

Make the card base from white card and glue the various parts on as shown. Tease out the cotton wool snow and apply to the glue gently. Glitter can be added as snowflakes, snow clinging to the brick face and as sparkle to the cotton wool, or as a glittered border all round the card edge. You can cut the sides of the card into a zigzag for added interest.

Dazzlingly bright wrapping-paper

What you need

Large sheets of thin poster paper (white or coloured), paint and glitter in assorted colours, saucers, pieces of flat sponge, potatoes, scissors, a craft knife, glue pens.

41

What to do

Cut the potatoes in half as evenly as possible to give a good, flat surface. Cut simple seasonal shapes such as trees, stars, bells and boxes into the halves, using a craft knife (an adult should do this). Leave a selection of bits of potato for the children to use. Let them make their own designs using one or more shapes. They can also decide their own colour scheme but, as they sometimes get overawed by choice, you may prefer to limit the number of shapes or colours per group of artists.

Sponge is a little difficult to shape but triangles make good trees and the children can attempt to cut bits of sponge themselves. Use the sponge in the same way as potato blocks, dipping into a saucer of paint, wiping off excess and printing carefully.

To add a little excitement to the design, wait for the paint to dry and draw different lines (straight, wavy, zigzag) with a glue pen all over the sheet. Sprinkle with glitter (see Glitzy wrapping-paper on page 41).

Marbled wrapping-paper

What you need

A large washing-up bowl, a selection of enamel paints (Humbrol) or other oil-based paints, strong white paper, small paintbrushes, white spirit, cloths, water, newspaper.

What to do

Fill the bowl half-full of water. Mix each paint well. Using the paintbrush, take a small brushful of paint and place it on the water surface. The paint will spread out into swirls of colour. Using a different

brush, add another colour to the surface, perhaps placing several dots of paint. The colours will swirl together sometimes. You can use as many colours as you like until the effect is pleasing.

To take a print, hold a sheet of paper with both hands and carefully lower it on to the surface of the water. The paint patterns will adhere to the surface of the paper.

Hold up the edge of the paper with the tip of an old pencil and lift it out carefully. Lay it out on newspaper to dry overnight.

The surface of the water should be almost clear after a print is taken. To clean it, draw strips of newspaper across the surface until all the paint has been removed.

The sheets can be used as wrapping-paper for smaller presents – or cut them into small rectangles and use as a background for silhouette Christmas shapes which can then be mounted on a card.

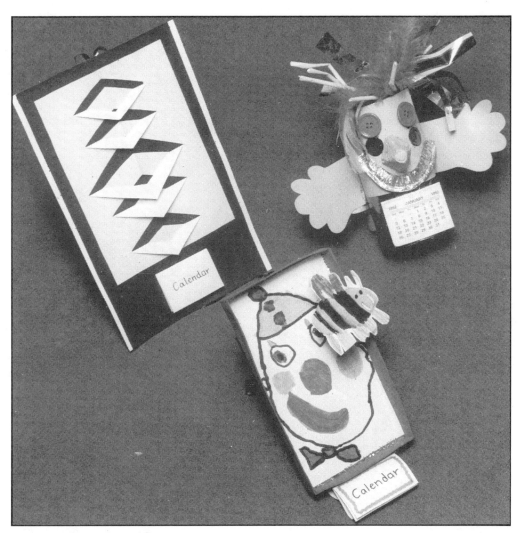

Calendars

Chapter five

As calendars decorate the home for a whole year, we have presented seasonally neutral ideas in a range of different media. For a change, some of the calendars are 3-D and can be set on a window-sill or shelf. One of the calendars needs to be in a window or near another source of light to show off its transparent colours to perfection. We have included different techniques such as clay work, drawing and card construction, and plenty of opportunity for the children to make a statement with individual design.

A family bus trip

What you need

A small cardboard box, white paper, a calendar book, photographs of the child's family (a head-and-shoulders cut-out of each member), PVA adhesive, paint, a black felt-tipped pen, scissors, wheels (strong card discs, bottle tops, jar lids etc.).

What to do

Seal the box by gluing white paper over the open end. Next, paint the box all over with a mixture of PVA and paint (two parts adhesive to one part paint). This helps the paint stick to glossier surfaces and prevents flaking. It also helps to cover any print. Leave to dry thoroughly, preferably overnight.

Cut a strip of paper long enough to go round two long sides and one short side of the bus and wide enough to form the windows. Draw pen lines across the paper to divide it up into windows and stick it in position with the adhesive.

For passengers, cut out the photographs and stick one in each window space with the child as the driver at the front. If no photographs are available, magazine cut-outs are just as suitable. To finish the bus, stick the wheels on, slightly away from each corner. Attach the calendar book in one of the windows.

Our house

What you need

A small cardboard box, coloured card or corrugated card, cardboard tubes, white paper, coloured papers, a calendar book, photos of the family members (a full-length one of the child and head-and-shoulder cut-outs of the other members) or cut-out pictures from catalogues or magazines, paint, PVA adhesive, scissors.

What to do

Paint the box as for the calendar bus (see above). Cut out paper windows and doors of an appropriate size and glue them to the box. Draw the child's house number on the door and glue the photos and the calendar book in the windows.

A self-portrait in a gilt frame

What you need

The lid of a child's shoebox, gold spray-paint, glitter, white paper, felt-tipped pens, coloured paper or Vivella, a calendar book, a small mirror, a piece of sequin strip or shiny parcel ribbon, sticky tape, adhesive, scissors.

What to do

Spray the back, the outsides and the inside edges, but not the inside lid, with gold paint (an adult should do this). Take care to do this in a well-ventilated area. Paint the open edge with adhesive and coat it well with glitter. You can sprinkle it on or dip the glued edges in a shallow container of glitter.

Cut a piece of Vivella or coloured paper deep enough to hold the calendar book and wide enough to fit inside the bottom part of the lid. Now you need a piece of white paper big enough to fit in the remaining space, on which the children can draw a self-portrait with felt-tipped pens. Small mirrors will aid the drawing as the children need to see what they look like.

Stick the portrait in the top part and the Vivella-mounted calendar book underneath it. To complete the picture frame, fix a loop of ribbon or a sequin strip to the back at the top of the frame, using sticky tape.

The child's own photo can be fixed to the door.

To make the roof, cut a piece of card as long as the house and as wide as would make a tall enough pitched roof. Score and fold along its length and bend it into shape. Spread adhesive along the long edges of the box and sit the roof on top of the box. You may need to hold it in place so use a quick-setting contact adhesive such as Copydex.

To complete the house, make a chimney from a small piece of cardboard tube. Cut a 'V' shape on either side of the bottom to fit over the arch of the roof and glue in place.

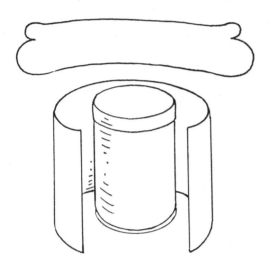

A calendar man

What you need

A cylindrical container (cocoa or gravy type), a calendar book, assorted colour paper, junk materials (buttons, feathers, bottle tops, wool, fabric bits), Copydex adhesive, scissors.

What to do

Cut out a piece of coloured paper to fit round the tin and glue it in place. Next, you can either cut out arms from coloured paper (see illustration) or let the child pick a piece of scrap material to use. Add another piece of fabric or paper around the lower part of the body. Glue the calendar back on to the lower half.

Any scrap material can be glued on to make the hair and the features. You can cut, tear, break, bend or stretch these materials to suit your purposes. Do remember that contact adhesives like Copydex work most effectively if the glue is put on both surfaces to be joined and left to dry a little before they are pressed together. It is especially important where items are to be stuck on a vertical surface.

A monoprint masterpiece

What you need

White or coloured sugar paper, white or coloured card, ready-mixed paint in assorted colours, coloured wool or metallic ribbon, a calendar book, PVA adhesive, sticky tape.

and let the children work it around, making lines, textures and patterns with their fingers. Children who can draw may want to do a picture of a face, a person, a house, a boat or any other simple line drawing; or they may prefer an abstract design. Squirts of different colours can be added and more lines made. Colours can also be mixed in this way.

When you are satisfied with your design, take a print by simply laying a piece of paper on top of the design and very gently smoothing it on to the paint below. Lift it off carefully and the design on the table surface should be transferred to the paper. If you mix PVA adhesive with the paint (two parts adhesive to one part paint), the dry print will have a glossy finish and a raised texture which is good to touch.

To produce a print which is the right size for your calendar, draw a rectangle or a circle in pencil on the printing surface and ask the children to try to keep the paint within this shape. Then lay the paper on top as before.

Try using different colours of paper and different shapes for the print and the mount, such as circles, rectangles, squares, diamonds, ovals. The language involved in selecting the shapes will certainly add to the children's maths experience.

To complete the calendar, mount the print with adhesive on a complementary colour of card, add a hanging loop and a calendar book fixed at the bottom with sticky tape.

What to do

With young children, monoprints are best done on a melamine or Formica surface. Squirt a patch of paint on to the surface

An everlasting calendar

What you need

Coloured card, white card, felt-tipped pens, spring-type clothes-pegs (stationers sometimes sell mini-ones which are better for this activity), coloured wool, sticky tape, adhesive, a pencil, a ruler, a calculator.

What to do

Cut a piece of coloured card about 50cm × 15cm to use as the base. Now cut a piece of white card 48cm × 13cm on which the information is to be written.

Obviously an adult will need to mark out the divisions for the calendar and a thin black felt-tipped pen is most effective for this purpose. Take just under half the length for the days-of-the-week section and the remainder for the months and dates. A calculator will help divide the space evenly. You will also need to leave a margin of 2cm at top and bottom for attaching the sheet to the backing. You can decorate the margin with a pattern.

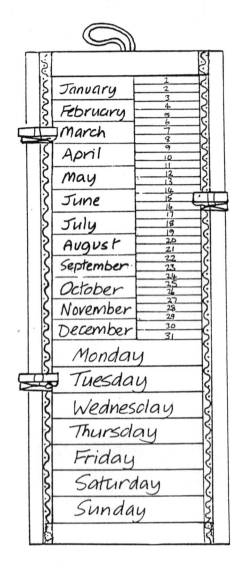

To mark out the details of days, months and dates (1 to 31) on the calendar, you may find it most effective to do each item at a different session as concentration span for new writers is limited. Each section can be written in a different colour.

To make up the calendar, tape a piece of wool to the reverse for a hanging loop and glue the information card to the backing card. A 1cm strip of adhesive at top and bottom is sufficient and leaves enough space for the pegs to be moved.

Clip the pegs to the sides as shown on the illustration. To use the calendar, just move the pegs daily to the correct information.

A paper sculpture calendar

What you need

Black card, white paper, a hanging loop, a calendar book, scissors, adhesive, sticky tape.

What to do

Paper sculpture requires not only paper-cutting skills but paper-handling ones such as making folds, creases, loops, bends, curls and concertinas. An abstract work such as this one gives the children an opportunity to try out and practise different skills.

Using white paper, let the children cut a variety of shapes, as much as possible by themselves, although they can still make the sculpture if the art of cutting eludes them at present. For example, they might cut thin or thick strips, rectangles, abstract shapes, curves, spirals and circles. The latter two are very difficult but we only learn by practice! Try drawing circles on scraps of paper for the children to cut along the lines, as well as letting them try free-hand ones.

Once you have a small collection of collage pieces, start sticking them to a sheet of white card about 18cm square, to make a 3-D design. The artists can decide on composition but encourage them to try the following:
- a loop – a long, thin piece stuck with a blob of adhesive at one end, and the other end glued in a different place to form a straight or curved line;
- a concertina – a long, thin line, folded into even concertinas and each end anchored with glue;
- a fan – a rectangle folded into a concertina with one end stapled, the other spread out;
- a cone – a circle of paper cut across the diameter to the centre, with the two cut edges pulled across each other to form a cone;
- an abstract – a torn piece of paper creased haphazardly and opened out, to be stuck down in any way.

To make the calendar, mount the card on a piece of folded black card with the calendar book mounted at the bottom.

A collage calendar

What you need

Tissue-paper shapes, white card, stiff card, PVA adhesive, glue brush or spreader, a calendar book, scissors.

What to do

Cut a circle of strong white card about 20cm in diameter. Select tissue paper shapes. (These shapes can be bought ready-cut.) Stick them on to the card circle in an abstract form or a regular pattern, but overlapping the shapes.

Using a brush or a wide glue spreader, cover the design with PVA adhesive to give a thin, even coating. The adhesive helps merge some colours and heighten them all and when it dries, it gives a glossy finish.

To construct the stand, use a long rectangle of stiff card, folded into a triangle shape, then glued to the back of the circle. Stick the calendar book at the bottom of the coloured design.

An antique metal plaque

What you need

A large tin-foil pie plate, an old ball-point pen or a thick pencil, red or blue shoe polish, tissue paper, white card, scissors, pinking shears, a folded newspaper, cloths, adhesive, sticky tape.

What to do

Cut the rim from the pie plate – pinking shears give an interesting zigzag edge. Rest the foil circle on a folded newspaper and draw a picture or a design, using a ball-point pen or a pencil. Work slowly with careful pressure to produce a well-defined line. The foil is quite fluid to work on. Turn the circle over to see the design in its raised and reversed form.

Wipe over the raised side with a coloured shoe polish and leave to dry overnight. Polish it with a cloth to reveal the raised areas and some of the base. This seems to highlight the raised pattern.

the card in an abstract pattern of creases and folds. Press down well round the edges and trim off neatly.

Stick the metal plaque in the centre of the tissue background. To complete, fix a calendar book to the bottom and a loop to the top, using sticky tape.

A stained-glass window

What you need

Clear and coloured acetate film, PVA adhesive, stiff black card, a calendar book, scissors, sticky tape.

What to do

Take a piece of stiff black card about 20cm × 15cm and cut out a window frame, leaving a border of about 2cm. Cut a support piece as wide as the frame and 1cm longer than the space from the bottom of the frame to the start of the window space. An adult will need to do all the preparation work for this activity.

Cut a piece of clear acetate film a bit larger than the window hole. Now cut or tear petals and leaves for the flower from coloured acetate film. Cut a centre from another colour. Stick them carefully to the clear acetate film with tiny spots of adhesive in key places. The edges of the petals and leaves can be left free if desired. The centre can be covered in adhesive as this is an anchor point and the adhesive will dry colourless. However, it will not be as clear as the unglued acetate film and we want to see as much clear colour as possible.

The support bracket can be fixed to the back of the window with sticky tape and the calendar book glued to the front part.

Mount the plaque on a contrasting textured background as follows. Take a circle of white card about 10cm wider than the plate base. Spread adhesive all over the card. Take a much larger sheet of tissue paper and let it fall on to the adhesive-covered card. Gently tugging and pulling the tissue, press it down on to

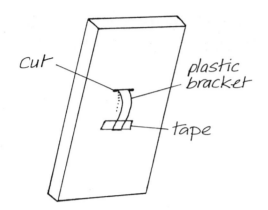

Bouncing bits

What you need

A shoe-box lid, white paper, a plastic drinks bottle, scissors, sticky tape, adhesive, coloured wool for hanging, a calendar book, gold spray-paint or ready-mixed paint, felt-tipped pens, a craft knife.

What to do

Paint or spray the back, sides and inner sides of the box lid. Cut a rectangle of white paper to fit inside the box. Draw a picture such as a clown's face or a flower-filled garden on the rectangle. The picture can be horizontal or vertical. On another piece of paper, draw some other item which could be part of the main picture, such as a bee buzzing round the clown's nose or a butterfly hovering over the flowers. Cut this small motif out. These can be fixed by a bouncing bracket to the main picture.

To make the bracket, cut up a plastic drinks bottle as shown on page 64 and cut a small strip 1cm to 0.5cm wide and about 10cm long. Tape one end of this to the back of the small motif.

Now glue the large picture into the box lid, covering all the back of the sheet with the adhesive. Allow to dry thoroughly. Next, hold the motif against the picture and gauge where the bracket

should be anchored to allow the motif to dangle where it looks best. Using the craft knife, make a small horizontal cut in the picture to go right through the box. An adult will need to do this and the mounting of the motif.

Push the end of the bracket through the hole and pull it down behind until it hangs in the right position over the main picture, then secure it with sticky tape. The bee will bounce over the clown's nose!

To complete, add a hanging loop and attach the calendar book underneath the picture with sticky tape.

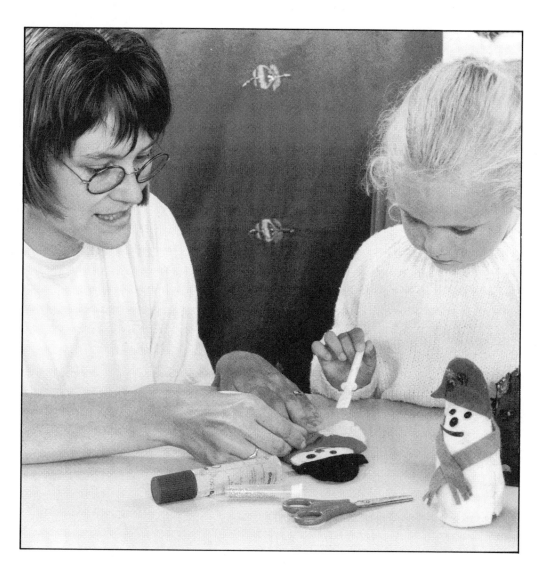

Presents

Chapter six

The activities in this section offer ideas for an exciting variety of presents. Although time is often at a premium in the festive season, careful planning in advance will allow the children a choice of three or four presents to make. The work could then be undertaken in groups if you organise and complete one set of presents at a time. The techniques include collage with natural and man-made materials, wood work, 3-D modelling with scraps and paint work.

A snowstorm

What you need

A small round jar with a tight-fitting lid, a small packet of plaster of Paris, two or three small twigs, half a tablespoon glitter, a plastic cake decoration, for example, a Father Christmas or a snowman, one teaspoon, cold boiled water to fill the jar.

What to do

Make up half of the packet of plaster of Paris and spoon it into the bottom of the jar. Just before it sets press the twigs and the cake decoration into it and firm them into place with the spoon so that they do not wobble. Leave it overnight for the plaster to harden. Add the cold boiled water so that you almost fill the jar and put in the glitter. Screw the lid on and shake the jar gently to create the snowstorm.

A pomander

What you need

An orange, 1.25m of cord or ribbon, cloves, allspice and cinnamon, a muslin square, a ball-point or a felt-tipped pen, scissors.

What to do

Begin by making channels for the ribbon: draw around the orange with a ball-point or felt-tipped pen so the lines act as a guide to follow when you press the cloves in. Form a second groove in the same way at right angles to the first.

The orange will now have four quarters outlined and these can be filled with cloves. When the orange is covered

all over (except in the grooves), tie the ribbon in place. The orange should now be hung in a warm, dry place for a week or two to dry out.

be given as a present to be hung in a wardrobe. Remember to allow plenty of time for this activity – at least three weeks for the complete process.

A jewelled paperweight

What you need

A large flat stone about the size of a large potato, large sequins, glass jewels or shiny buttons, clear varnish in a spray (Humbrol), strong adhesive, glitter.

What to do

To turn the stone into an attractive paperweight, stand the pebble on a piece of paper and cover the top and sides thickly with the adhesive. Drop the sequins or glass jewels on to the adhesive as close together as possible, then sprinkle glitter into the spaces between and leave it to dry. When it is thoroughly dry, take it outside and spray with clear varnish. An adult should closely supervise this activity, especially the final stages as it is dangerous to allow the children to handle aerosol sprays on their own. Make sure that the ventilation is good when handling the strong adhesive.

Lentils and peas sprayed gold or silver and sprinkled with glitter are just as effective if it is not possible to use the other materials.

Make a mixture of equal parts of allspice and cinnamon and sprinkle it over the pomander. Wrap it lightly in a cloth then leave in a warm dry place for another week. The pomander can then

A bookmark

What you need

Strips of felt 6cm × 20cm, circles of card 6cm in diameter, large sequins or glitter, strips of small sequins, small photographs cut from magazines or, if preferred, seasonal pictures cut from old Christmas cards, Copydex adhesive, scissors.

What to do

Take a circle of card and select one of the small pictures. Glue it to the centre of the card, making sure that the picture fits neatly. Then decorate all around the edge of the picture and the card with sequins or glitter. When dry, stick the circle on to the strip of felt at the top. The bottom edge of the bookmark can either be fringed or cut to a point. If desired, the top and bottom edges can be trimmed with a row of small sequins.

A desk tidy

What you need

Strong card for the base, a collection of cardboard tubes, paint, small pictures or patterns cut from sticky-backed plastic or small pictures from magazines, clear varnish, PVA adhesive, scissors.

What to do

Cut the cardboard tubes to different heights and cut a circle 20cm in diameter from the strong card. Glue three of the tubes to the base card as shown in the illustration.

Paint the tubes and the card and leave to dry. The tubes can then be decorated

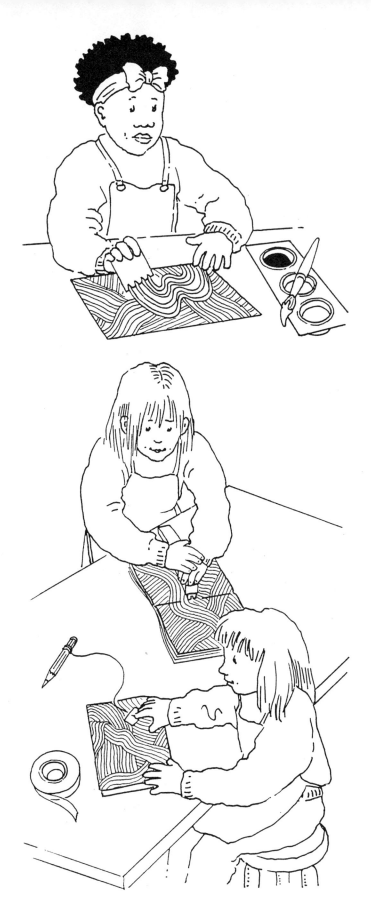

with the pictures and patterns. To finish off, the desk tidy can be given a coat of PVA adhesive or sprayed with clear varnish for protection. An adult should perform the spray-painting outside to avoid the children breathing in any vapours, and the room should be well ventilated if using strong adhesive.

A decorated notebook

What you need

Cartridge paper, stiff card, several sheets of blank paper, a pencil, a length of wool or cord, a stapler, PVA adhesive, paint, scissors.

What to do

Mix the paint with an equal quantity of PVA adhesive to a really thick consistency. Prepare several pots of the mixture in assorted colours. To make the cover, take a sheet of cartridge paper 20cm × 20cm and cover it on one side with two colours of paint. Make a comb from stiff card by taking a small rectangle and cutting ridges in the bottom edge as shown.

Place the cut edge on the painted paper and make patterns by dragging the comb backwards and forwards over the surface. Leave it to dry. Take several sheets of blank paper, the same size as the cover, lay them on top of each other and fold them down the middle — these are the pages of the notebook. Take the painted cover and fold it down the middle. Place the blank sheets inside the cover and staple them in the middle. If you like, attach a pencil to the book by taping a length of cord or wool to the back cover and tying the pencil to the other end.

A vase of dried flowers

What you need

Cardboard tubes, modelling clay, dried flowers or grasses, dried oak or birch leaves, gold spray-paint, crinkled foil, scissors, adhesive.

What to do

Take the cardboard tube and cut a piece of crinkled foil large enough to roll it in. Wrap the foil around the tube and glue it in place. Tuck the ends of the foil down the inside of the tube. Take a few of the dried leaves and spray them gold. When dry, glue them to the front of the cardboard tube as a decoration. You can add one or two of the smaller dried flowers as well.

Take a lump of modelling clay and place it at the bottom of the tube to act as a weight. The amount of clay used will depend on the size of the finished arrangement. Now choose some of the dried grasses and flowers and make a small posy to fit into the decorated vase. Press the stems gently into the clay.

A decorated box

What you need

A soft margarine container, felt in assorted colours, lace, buttons, sequins, shells, Polyfilla, adhesive, scissors.

What to do

Most soft margarine containers are attractively decorated already. The lids usually bear the trade name and this needs to be covered. Draw around the lid on a piece of coloured felt and cut out. Cover the lid with glue and stick the felt on. The felt can be decorated with any of the small items mentioned and a length of lace can be stuck round the edge to finish it off. The box can be used to store anything from paper-clips and drawing pins to peanuts or sweets.

Alternatively, you can cover the lid with Polyfilla and decorate with attractive stones, shells or small pine cones while the Polyfilla is still soft. This can be sprayed gold when dry.

A dog-lead holder

What you need

A photograph of the dog whose lead is going to hang on the holder or, if this is

and fasten coloured twine between them so that the holder can be hung on the wall. Finally, make two holes with a bradawl just below the dog's picture and screw in the two cup hooks, one for the dog lead and the other to hang the dog brush.

Bookends

What you need

Tin cans with lids that can be replaced, for example, the kind that holds milk powder or instant mashed potato, sand, adhesive tape, pieces of felt and fabric in assorted colours (make sure you have some flesh-coloured felt for the faces and hands), scraps of lace and ribbon, wool, Copydex adhesive, buttons.

What to do

First of all, fill the tins with sand and use the adhesive tape to secure the lids tightly. Take a strip of flesh-coloured felt, enough to cover about halfway down from the top of the tin. Glue the felt in place on the tin. Cut out the eyes, nose and mouth from felt and stick them on. Take a strip of patterned fabric for the dress, enough to cover the rest of the tin down to the bottom. Decorate the dress with scraps of lace or ribbon, and add one or two buttons down the front. Cut long strips of felt and glue them in place for the arms and legs. Finish these off with hand shapes and shoes cut out from felt and glue these in place. Cut the wool into lengths of about 25cm and glue them to the top of the figures to represent hair. If you would like to make boy and girl figures, style the hair shorter and longer, respectively.

not possible, a magazine picture showing the same or similar breed, a piece of wood at least 5cm larger than the photograph all the way round, sandpaper, wood stain, brushes, cup hooks, two small nails, hammer, bradawl, coloured twine, adhesive, clear varnish, brush, aprons, rubber gloves.

What to do

This activity will need close supervision and a lot of adult help throughout.
   Sand the wood until it is smooth and stain with the wood stain. Make sure the children are wearing aprons and, if possible, rubber gloves. Leave the block to dry. Glue the photograph to the centre of the block. Make sure the adhesive is really dry and varnish the wooden block and the photograph. When dry, hammer two small nails into the sides of the block

Pasta necklaces

What you need

Pasta shapes (any kind that can be threaded), wooden beads, a plastic needle, thick poster paint, scissors, rolled elastic, clear varnish, a paintbrush.

What to do

Take some of the pasta shapes and paint them with thick poster paint. Leave to dry. When the paint is completely dry, brush the pasta shapes with clear varnish or spray with varnish. Remember to use the varnish in a well-ventilated place. Cut a piece of rolled elastic a little longer than you want the necklace to be. Thread it on to a plastic needle and start to thread the pasta tubes and wooden beads in an alternating row. When the necklace is complete, tie the ends of the elastic in a knot. Older children can use a bodkin needle to thread different pasta shapes on to the elastic. Smaller children can thread large chunky pasta shapes or beads on to a length of thin ribbon. The ends of the ribbon can then be tied in a bow to complete the necklace.

A Christmas pudding tea-cosy and egg-cosies

What you need

Red, green, white, tan and black felt, Copydex adhesive, scissors.

What to do

Tea-cosies and egg-cosies can add a festive touch to the breakfast table on

Christmas morning. The Christmas pudding tea-cosy and the egg-cosies are easy to make from felt.

and glue them in place. Stick small circles of black felt on the exposed tan section to represent the currants and decorate the top with two green-felt holly leaves and three red-felt holly berries.

The egg-cosies are made in the same way. The tree can be decorated with sequins and glitter and the snowman can be given shiny sequins for eyes.

A wall hanging

What you need

A rectangle of hessian or felt, a length of dowelling, a selection of dried grasses and flowers, card or string, Copydex adhesive, scissors.

What to do

Cut a rectangle of felt or hessian to the size you want the wall hanging to be. Take a length of dowelling about 6cm longer than the width of your wall hanging, so that there are at least three centimetres of dowelling sticking out on either side. Roll the top of the material over the dowelling so that the edge can be glued to the back of the hanging.

Remove the dowelling and decorate the front of the material with the dried grasses and flowers. Replace the dowelling rod and attach the length of string or cord to the protruding ends of the rod.

Variation: The same idea can be used to create a wall plaque. Take a clean polystyrene tray and spray it gold. Cut a piece of material or coloured paper large enough to cover the bottom of the inside of the tray and stick it in place with adhesive. The tray can now be decorated in the same way as the wall hanging, and an opened paper-clip fixed to the back with sticky tape can be used to hang it up.

Cut two pudding shapes from tan felt, large enough to cover a standard-sized teapot. Glue around the curved edges leaving free the bottom straight edge, a section at the front of the shape for the spout to go through and a section at the back for the handle to go through. Cut two white felt shapes to represent sauce

A key tidy

What you need

A wooden spoon, a roll of patterned Fablon or sticky-backed plastic (flowers or geometric patterns are best), three cup hooks, strong cord, scissors, a bradawl.

What to do

The wooden spoon can either be painted or left the natural wood colour. Choose the patterns you like best and cut them from the roll of sticky-backed plastic. (The children will need some help with peeling off the protective sheet at the back.) Decorate the spoon as you like, by sticking the cut-out motifs on. When the spoon is decorated, make three holes along the handle with a bradawl or other sharp instrument. Screw the cup hooks in place. Make sure that all the hooks are pointing the right way up and add a loop of cord for the key tidy to hang by.

A coin paperweight

What you need

A good selection of coins – foreign coins left over from a holiday, old coins from pre-decimal times, or tokens sometimes given by garages and shops as a special promotion; a piece of strong cardboard, strong adhesive, PVA adhesive or clear varnish.

What to do

Cut the card the size and shape you want the paperweight to be. Cover one side with the strong adhesive. Remember to have good ventilation during this activity. Stick down the largest coins as close

together as possible, with their edges overlapping the edge of the cardboard. When the whole of the card has been covered, glue more layers of coins on top. When completely dry, the paperweight can be given a coating of PVA adhesive or clear varnish for protection.

Hats, masks and costumes

Chapter seven

These items can be made for play, drama productions or as party wear. Children love dressing up, and it is worth taking care to make their dressing-up clothes fit well.

There are five types of headgear suitable for this age group:
- the circlet – a band which goes around the head;
- the face – worn like a circlet but showing a full face;
- the mask – covering the whole face, leaving eye holes;
- the full head – covering the head, leaving eye holes;
- the hat – which sits on top of head.

All have to be carefully fitted so that they don't annoy the child and/or fall off.

Basic designs

The following items are used in several of the ideas for hats and masks, so they have been described below to save repetition.

To make a circlet, cut a band of card about 4cm × 60cm and fit it round the child's head as shown. Staple this fitting and cut off the excess card.

To make a bouncing bracket, take a large plastic drinks bottle and cut off the top and the bottom. Now cut down the bottle vertically to open it out. Strips to be used as brackets can be cut widthways across the bottle as if it were a Swiss roll. The width of these strips can vary and the length can be adjusted when assembling the model.

A golden halo

What you need

Card, gold foil paper, glitter, a pencil, adhesive, scissors.

What to do

Cut a circle of card about 25cm in diameter and two circles of gold foil the same size. Stick the gold on either side of the card.

To make the head hole, take a strip of card about 60cm long and fit it round the child's head fixing the ends temporarily with a paper-clip. Sit it on the card circle, slightly off-centre, and mark the inside of the circle with a pencil. Cut out the circle. If the hole is too small, it can be enlarged slightly to fit.

To complete the halo, hold it by the inside ring and paint adhesive along the edge so that both sides have a covering. Dip the edge in a saucer of glitter. It is best to do small sections at a time.

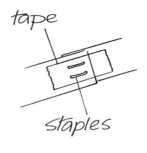

All staples on the inside of a hat must be covered with tape.

A starshine circlet

What you need

Gold or white card circlet, gold, silver or blue foil, a stapler, adhesive, scissors.

Fix the stars point-to-point around the band with a blob of adhesive in the centre of each.

A robin in the evergreens

What you need

A circlet of white or gold card, green and red foil, green sugar paper, white paper, felt-tipped pens, scissors, a stapler, a bouncing bracket, adhesive.

What to do

Make a circlet of card as described opposite. Next, cut out a large number of holly and ivy leaves from green foil and green sugar paper. Children who are able to cut their own can use stencils. Make the leaves about 10cm at their longest.

Using the white paper and the felt-tipped pens, the children can draw a robin and cut it out themselves too, if possible. The bird should be about 10cm from nose to tail.

Make a bouncing bracket (see opposite) and staple the robin to one end. You will need to experiment with the length of the bracket by trying on the circlet and moving the bracket up and down to see which length looks best. Staple the bracket in position, with the robin dangling on the outside of the circlet.

To fix the leaves on the circlet, first glue a selection of flat leaves all around. Then fold some of the leaves down the middle for a 3-D effect and stick these over the flat leaves, using a little adhesive on the back. The final effect should be a profusion of leaves in a mixture of dull and shiny green. Add a few circles of red foil for holly berries, scattered in bunches around the circlet.

What to do

Make the circlet as shown opposite. Cut enough stars from the foil to fit all round it. Make the stars about 6cm across, slightly wider than the band.

Children who are able can draw round a star stencil and cut out their own stars, or at least one or two of them. For those more dextrous with scissors, fold a strip of foil into four and show them how to cut out four stars at once by holding the paper firmly and keeping it in place as it is turned and cut.

A royal crown

What you need

A circlet of gold- or silver-covered card, six bouncing brackets, glitter, assorted colours of foil paper, adhesive, scissors.

What to do

Make a circlet of gold card 10cm wide (as shown on page 64) and cut zigzags along one edge. Now make six bouncing brackets (also shown on page 64) long enough to hang over the edge of the circlet. Spread them evenly round the circlet and staple on the inside with the staple opening on the outside.

Cut a selection of 4cm circles in coloured foil and glue one over each of the staples showing on the front of the circlet. Add one of these 'jewels' to the end of each of the brackets and stick another one in contrasting colour to the reverse so that both colours can be seen as the brackets bounce round the wearer's head.

The artist may feel the whole ensemble needs glitter to complete it. This can be added along the edges of the brackets or around the edge of the 'jewels'.

The evening star

What you need

A circlet of gold or black card, gold card, gold glitter, a doily, Copydex adhesive, a bouncing bracket, sticky tape, scissors.

What to do

Make a circlet from gold or black card (see page 64) and staple a single bouncing bracket about 4cm wide on to it (see page 64). Spread a thin strip of

adhesive carefully along the centre line of the circlet and cover with glitter.

Cut out a 10cm star in gold card and make a glitter pattern on it as follows: place the doily over the star and, using Copydex (which leaves a tight pattern and does not dribble), paint adhesive into the holes of the doily. Remove the doily gently and sprinkle the glue pattern with the glitter. Leave to dry thoroughly.

To finish the circlet, use sticky tape to fix the back of the star to the bracket.

Animals and birds

What you need

A circlet of white card, any other colour card, foil paper, coloured acetate film, pipe cleaners, art straws, twigs, wool, scissors, felt-tipped pens, adhesive.

What to do

Make a circlet of card (see page 64) and add eyes and nose or beak by cutting card to the appropriate shape. This can be painted, coloured with felt-tipped pens or covered with foil or coloured acetate film. Additional decorations such as whiskers can be made with art straws, pipe cleaners or twigs. Antlers can be made with twigs, and feathers and paper curls or unravelled wool added for feathers or hair.

A party-time mask

What you need

Any colour card, assorted small decorative items (feathers, sequins, buttons, ribbons, paper scraps, threads), adhesive, scissors, a stapler.

What to do

Cut out the shape of the mask as shown and a strip of card 3cm × 40cm. Cut out the eye holes. Staple one end of the strip inside the edge of the mask, fit to the wearer's head and staple the other end.

To decorate the mask, stick on any of the small items, either at random or in regular patterns. Items can be stuck on to the mask front or allowed to stick out over the sides or above the nose. You could also attach ribbons or curls of paper to hang down from the sides.

A second face

What you need

A circlet of card (see page 64), card, assorted scraps for decoration, wax crayons, a clear wax candle, paint, sticky tape, a stapler, adhesive, scissors.

What to do

Draw a 20cm circle of card and add a smaller semicircle on each side for ear shapes. Cut this out. Using wax crayons, draw the features but no hair. As this is to be part of the wax-and-wash process, press on very hard with the crayons to get a good covering of wax. You can go over the features with a clear wax candle to help the technique succeed. Now go over the face with a light wash of paint, depending on the artist's own skin colour or preference. He or she may fancy a green face!

Using scrap materials, you can now add hair (wool, raffia, shredded paper, straws, curled paper strips, cotton wool etc.). You could also add other interesting details such as a card or cloth bow, a hat cut from card, a crown made from a row of milk-bottle tops, a glitter or cotton-wool beard, earrings and so on.

To turn the flat face into a hat, simply staple, tape or glue it to the card circlet. Fix it on to the curve at about a third of the way down the circle of the face. This ensures that it sits on the child's head like a sun visor and doesn't restrict vision, but can easily be seen by other children.

68

rabbits, bears, dogs or cats. These can be cut out of card by the children themselves if skills permit and stapled, glued or taped into position.

Use straws, pipe cleaners or twigs for whiskers and glue these under noses made from bottle tops, buttons, circles of black paper, egg-box spacers and so on.

Eyes drawn with black felt-tipped pens look quite effective. Remember to draw them quite large and leave a triangle of white in the pupil to add sparkle.

Simple hats

What you need

Large sheets of paper or card, crêpe paper, wool, raffia, an assortment of scraps for decoration, ribbing elastic, ribbon, adhesive, scissors.

What to do

There are two simple hat shapes which the children can help make and decorate themselves.

The first is a cone of any size, either to fit over the head or to sit perched on top. You need a semicircle to make it. The most effective anchor for a small cone is ribbing elastic stapled to the hat or, for a large cone, ribbon ties stapled to each side and tied under the chin.

The second is an open triangle, the top part of which can be cut to any shape, as shown. It is made of two sheets glued together at the sides. This can be fitted to the head and perched in place or anchored in the same way as the cone.

Both types of hats can be decorated in a free style by the artists, gluing on whatever takes their fancy. Some sort of streamers or ribbons are perennially popular and can be made from crêpe paper, raffia or wool.

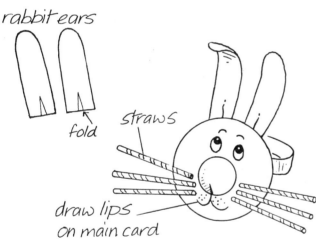

Variations on the face hat

What you need

The same materials as in the previous activity plus felt-tipped pens.

What to do

Make the face in the same way but leave off the ear shapes for variations on the theme. Add suitably shaped ears for

A knight of the realm

What you need

Large sheets of card, silver or gold foil paper, paper fasteners, coloured paper, adhesive, sticky tape, a stapler, scissors.

What to do

Cut a piece of card about 25cm × 60cm. Cover it with foil using the adhesive spread thinly all over. Shape into a cylinder to fit on to the child's head, leaving it large enough to let the head turn comfortably inside it. Fix with staples and cut off the excess card. Add a strip of sticky tape to cover the staples inside and out.

Now cut a vision hole in the front of the helmet. This should be round the level of the child's eyes, about 16cm × 7cm. Make a visor as shown, with the same-size vision hole, and fix it to the helmet using paper fasteners on either side of the top of the hole. You will need to bell the visor out before fixing so that it can be lifted up over the cylinder.

To complete, add a paper plume. Roll a piece of coloured paper fairly tightly, then cut down the top of the roll to make strips. Pull the centre out to form a 'palm tree' effect and tape in position.

You could use the same basic design to make a diver's or an astronaut's helmet. For a diver's helmet, add an acetate film window stuck to the inside of the eye space. Attach a cocoa-tin lid to each side for pressure valves. Any flexible plastic tubing can be taped to the underside of the front and draped over the shoulder, then fixed inside the back.

For an astronaut, use white card for the helmet and paint an assortment of scraps white before sticking them on to represent valves and gauges. Decorate with a couple of strips of colour and add a national flag or a logo.

Skirts and cloaks from crêpe paper

What you need

Assorted colours of crêpe paper, coloured card, glitter, assorted colours of paint, scrap items for printing with, Copydex adhesive, a stapler, scissors, sticky tape, large safety pins, ribbon.

What to do

The following are a few suggestions for simple costumes which the children can help make.

Decorating the crêpe

Unroll a complete roll (about 2m) of crêpe paper on to a large table so that it can be worked on and secure each end to the table with tape.

For printing, use small scrap items such as kitchen-roll ends, pastry cutters, glue spreaders, box ends etc, and paint. Take care not to get the paper too wet or to overload the design as crêpe paper is delicate. Let it dry thoroughly.

For glitter-and-glue printing, print with well-defined items, spreading the design out or the paper will get too heavy to use. Copydex works best for glue prints. Print the whole sheet, then sprinkle over with glitter. Shake off the excess.

For glue dribbling with glitter, use a well-loaded glue spreader and let the glue dribble in thin lines all over the paper. Lines following the grain look particularly effective. Sprinkle glitter all over and shake off the excess.

Making up

To make a skirt, cut a piece of card 10cm wide and 15cm longer than the average child's waist measurement and fold it in half lengthwise. Spread the adhesive on the inside of one half and fit the edge of the crêpe paper as shown, ruching it up to fill the length of the card. Now spread a little adhesive along the outer edge of the free side of the card and fold it down onto the gathers and press firmly. Allow to dry and the skirt is complete. Any shaping can be cut before gathering (see illustration). To wear, wrap round the waist and secure at the back with a large safety pin. These items will last for more than one occasion if treated with respect.

To make a cloak, cut a necklet of card as shown on the illustration and spread with adhesive. Gather the edge of the crêpe paper on to the adhesive to fit round the shape. Cut a second matching necklet and glue it over the gathers to secure them. Staple ribbons to each open edge to fasten the cloak.

Decorating fabric

What you need

Old sheets, paint in assorted colours, different-sized paintbrushes, scrap printing items, a large plastic sheet, a stapler or sticky tape, scissors.

What to do

Fasten a plastic sheet to a wall or spread it on a large table and arrange half a single plain bedsheet on top, stretching it tight. If possible, staple or tape the sheet to the surface.

Decorate by printing a design with ordinary powder paint or by simply painting with a brush. Stripes look effective and can be used for shepherds' robes in the Nativity. More regal designs can be produced by adding just a border pattern, using gold paint. Vary the size of the brushes and experiment with the consistency of the paint as paint that is too thick produces very stiff cloth.

Use foil-paper shapes glued on with Copydex for royalty or magic characters.

Pictures

Chapter eight

Pictures need not be religious: seasonal pictures have a long classroom life and save time. Pictures in this chapter range from abstract to realistic and can be completed by groups of children or by individuals. Their size is up to you – for example, you can make a frieze of the winter evening pictures, including a house for everyone in the class; the thumb-print robins can be made into a selection of winter birds by using different colours on the birds. We include different painting techniques such as frottage and collage, and ideas for mounting pictures which show off the work to the best advantage.

A winter evening

What you need

Backing sheets of grey or pale-orange sugar paper, black and yellow paper, silver glitter, scissors, adhesive.

What to do

Cut the backing sheets to the desired size and then cut out a variety of different-sized rectangles and shapes for roofs, in black or in a darker-grey colour. You can make templates for these and those children who are able can stencil round them and cut out their own shapes.

These shapes can be used to make a town or city skyline. Lay them out on the backing paper before sticking them, until you have found the best arrangement. The shapes can overlap if you like.

To make lighted windows, cut out a few yellow rectangles and stick them on some of the buildings. Add a large orange sun in the sky.

To add a touch of frost, dab adhesive on the top edges of the rooftops and sprinkle with glitter.

To turn this picture into 'Christmas Eve in town' leave out the sun and substitute a gold sickle moon and some sequin stars to the grey night sky. Cut out a small Father Christmas from a Christmas card to stand in a rectangular chimney on a roof or a Father Christmas in his sleigh flying over the rooftops.

A stocking full of wishes

What you need

Christmas wrapping-paper, red parcel ribbon, white paper, felt-tipped pens or wax crayons, adhesive.

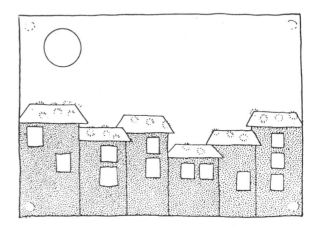

What to do

First of all, talk to the children about the custom of exchanging presents at Christmas. Ask what they would like to get and what they think members of their family would like. Ask them to think of the needs of poorer people for food, shelter or clothes.

To complete the picture, cut out stocking shapes from the wrapping-paper, about 5cm larger all round than the white stocking shapes, and mount the drawings on the fancy backing. Add a red ribbon bow at the top corner.

A Nativity scene (wax and wash)

What you need

Wax crayons, good-quality white paper, blue wash (blue paint thinned down), a large paintbrush or a sponge.

What to do

Look at pictures of the Nativity in books and on Christmas cards and ask the children to draw their favourite group or scene from the story. For this technique to produce an attractive effect, the wax needs to be applied quite thickly with a heavy hand. Encourage the children to use a variety of colour and to fill the page with the picture. A simple group such as the Holy Family in the stable or an angel is sometimes most effective.

Test the wash on a scrap of paper with some crayoned drawing before applying to the picture. If the paint runs off the waxed lines, leaving the colours bright and colouring the unwaxed paper sufficiently, then it is the correct consistency. Apply it with a large, soft brush or a sponge which should be stroked across the paper from side to side to give the cover. However, if it is scrubbed on with an ordinary paint brush by an enthusiastic infant, then the effect is sometimes more exciting!

Cut out stocking shapes from the white paper and ask the children to draw one or more presents on them. They can use pens or crayons. An adult can write the name of the objects drawn if the child wishes. Encourage the children to use as much colour as possible and to draw as large as possible with good detail. It helps to discuss the drawings as the children work.

A thumb-print picture

What you need

A rectangle of grey sugar paper 15cm × 20cm, brown, red, white and black poster paint, black sugar paper, felt-tipped pens, gold and silver foil, a drinking straw.

What to do

Take the rectangle of grey activity paper and drop a blob of black poster paint in the bottom left-hand corner. With the drinking straw, blow the paint away from the corner and the impression left by the paint as it is pushed along will look like bare branches of a tree. Make these branches as long as you can and try to blow little twigs off the main branch as you go along. Allow to dry, then dip your thumb into the brown paint. This is going to be the little robin sitting on a branch.

Press your thumb down so that it is sitting on one of the branches and leave a thumb-print. Now dip your little finger into the red paint for the robin's breast. When this is dry, draw in the robin's beak and eye and add a tail. Next cut out a circle of gold foil for the winter sun and add small spots of white paint to the grey background, for a gentle fall of snow. Mount the picture on a sheet of black sugar paper and trim with a zigzag of silver foil down each side.

Three fancy kings

What you need

Backing paper (any colour), assorted pieces of fabric, braids, ribbons, sequins, threads, feathers, glitter, coloured paper foil, sand, scissors, adhesive.

What to do

As cutting fabric is usually too difficult for most in this age group, cut out large triangles of fabric suitable for the body of

To complete the picture, paint adhesive down the bottom half of the picture and sprinkle with sand to represent the desert. You could also stick a foil star in the sky.

A 3-D snow scene

What you need

A shoe-box lid, gold spray-paint, grey sugar paper, white ready-mixed powder paint, a selection of old Christmas cards, narrow cardboard tubing cut into 3cm sections, Copydex adhesive, paintbrushes, scissors.

What to do

Spray the back and sides of the box lid with gold paint, leaving the inside of the lid bare. An adult should do this in a well-ventilated place, taking care that none of the spray goes on an unwanted surface or near a face.

Cut a piece of grey paper to fit inside the box lid. Older children can try to cut the paper themselves with guidance.

Paint snowy hills and falling snowflakes on the grey paper using the white paint. Let it dry before sticking it inside the box lid.

Cut out two or three Christmas figures and motifs from cards. For example, you could use snowmen, mice, teddy bears, Father Christmas, children, a couple of holly leaves, a Christmas tree and a robin. Stick a piece of cardboard tube to the centre back of each and, when dry, stick the tube backing of the figures in position on the snowy background. The tube lifts the figures away from the background to give a 3-D effect.

Notes

Alternatively, paint a desert background and use cut-outs of the Nativity story for the figures.

a king. You will also need to cut different colours for faces and an assortment of odd shapes and scraps for other details.

Let the children select three bodies and heads and place them on paper. Stick them in place with the adhesive.

The kings can now be decorated with scraps of fabric and foil for the crowns, head-dresses, arms, gifts, jewels and so on. Each bit can be stuck on as the artist selects it.

A frottage picture

What you need

Thin card, scissors, wax crayons, cartridge paper, adhesive.

What to do

Using the card, cut out a large star shape and small circles, strips, zigzags, waves, squares and triangles. Decorate the large star with the smaller shapes by gluing them on to it.

When the adhesive is dry, use the star to make crayon rubbings by placing it underneath a sheet of cartridge paper and rubbing the surface with the side of a wax crayon. As you do this the pattern will be revealed. Make sure you have got the whole shape and then move the card underneath the paper just a little bit and rub again, this time with a different-coloured crayon. Repeat this process several times to create an interestingly-textured picture.

Try decorating different shapes, such as a stocking, cracker, bell or tree.

The finished rubbing can be displayed side by side with the base card.

A Christmas painting

What you need

Assorted paints, paintbrushes, white paper, red or green backing paper, silver or gold foil paper, pastels in assorted colours, adhesive, scissors.

What to do

Discuss with the children what Christmas means to them and what pictures and feelings come to mind when they think of it. It may be an image of Father Christmas, the baby Jesus, a longed-for

present, a party dressing-up outfit, a Christmas tree and so on.

Now ask them to paint that picture on white paper, using as many colours as they can and filling the page. When this is dry, they can add details with pastels. For example, pastel decorations can be added to a painted tree. Features can be added to a face, a pattern to a dress or a parcel, lines of fur to an animal's coat, clouds drawn on a sky and so on. When using pastels, start working at the top of the page and work down as pastels smudge readily.

To complete the picture with a festive flourish, mount on red or green backing paper and add a row of silver-foil stars down the two vertical borders.

Cookery

Chapter nine

Cooking is as much an art form as painting or sculpting, as we want our food to look attractive and interesting. At the same time it is a branch of science as we combine, heat or freeze different ingredients. As we usually work in small groups for cookery, there is plenty of opportunity to develop scientific or design ideas and develop language, as well as producing an edible end product which can be tested on the spot.

The culinary ideas we offer in this section can be used for the school party, as presents, or for an impromptu class feast at break time or on a cold afternoon.

Chocolate medals

What you need

Ingredients: large bars of chocolate.

Equipment: sticky tape, coloured ribbons, coloured foil, a mixing bowl, a small saucepan, a plate, a wooden spoon, cake cases, scissors.

What to do

An adult will need to supervise this activity very closely, especially as boiling water is involved.

Break the chocolate up into a bowl. Heat some water in the saucepan until it is just beginning to boil. Stand the bowl over the saucepan on low heat and, when the chocolate begins to melt, stir it until smooth.

Put the cake cases on a plate and pour about 0.5cm of melted chocolate into each cake case. Put the cases in the fridge until they set hard. Remove the chocolate discs from paper cases and wrap each disc in coloured foil. Secure the foil at the back with the sticky tape. Next take a length of ribbon about 70cm long for each medal and bend it into a loop. Tape this to the back of each medal, so that it can be worn around the neck.

Fondant sweets

What you need

Ingredients: two cups of icing sugar, one egg white, flavourings and colourings.

Equipment: a sieve, two bowls, a whisk, a rounded knife, a plate.

What to do

Sieve the icing sugar into a bowl. Beat the egg white and pour it slowly into the icing sugar. Fold it in with a rounded knife, then knead it until it is well mixed

quantity of the fondant icing and, using food colourings, colour some red, some blue, some yellow, some green and some black. Use the red icing to make a nose. The scarf can be green or yellow and the eyes and buttons can be either blue or black. Finish it off with a black hat.

Pepparkakor biscuits

What you need

Ingredients: 400g flour, 1 teaspoon of bicarbonate of soda, 1½ teaspoons of mixed ground ginger, cloves and cinnamon, 230g butter or margarine, 230g dark brown sugar, 2 egg whites. For icing: 250g icing sugar, 1 egg white, candied fruit or silver balls for decoration.

Equipment: a sieve, two bowls, a wooden spoon, foil, a pastry board, a rolling pin, pastry cutters, a baking sheet.

What to do

Sift the flour, spices and bicarbonate of soda together. Mix the butter and sugar into a fluffy paste and beat in the egg whites. Slowly add the dry ingredients and work them all together. Wrap the mixture in foil and store in a cold place for about twelve hours. Heat the oven to 350 degrees F or Gas Mark 4. Roll out the dough about 0.5cm thick on a lightly floured board. Use the pastry cutters to cut out the shapes, and place them on an ungreased baking sheet leaving a space between each one. Place them in the oven and cook for 10 minutes or until light brown around the edges.

Take the biscuits out and, while they are cooling, you can prepare the icing. Make it stiff enough to pipe in chosen patterns on the biscuits. Decorate with silver balls or candied fruit.

together. This basic mixture can be flavoured with strawberry, coffee, almond or peppermint essence. Roll the mixture into small balls and flatten the tops. Leave them on a plate sprinkled with icing sugar to harden.

To make fondant snowmen, take two of the small balls and flatten them by pressing with your hand. Take a small

Marzipan sweets

What you need

Ingredients: 100g sifted icing sugar, 100g ground almonds, two teaspoons lemon juice, one egg white, food colouring, small sweets or nuts.

Equipment: a small jug, a mixing bowl, a wooden spoon, a rolling pin, a round-ended knife.

What to do

Mix the icing sugar and ground almonds together in a mixing bowl, using the wooden spoon. Beat the lemon juice and egg white together in a small jug. Add half the liquid to the mixture in the bowl and mix well. Add enough of the remaining liquid to turn the mixture into a stiff paste and knead until smooth. If the marzipan becomes too soft, add a little more icing sugar until it is the required texture. (For younger children use ready-made almond paste.) Add colour to the marzipan by pouring a few drops of food colouring into a small bowl, taking small pieces of marzipan and kneading them until they are evenly coloured. Roll out to the desired thickness. Use the pastry cutters to cut shapes and decorate with nuts or small sweets. The children can make all sorts of shapes and decorate them in lots of different ways using contrasting colours of marzipan.

Party dips

What you need

Dip ingredients (see below), mixing bowls, a chopping board, a knife, a wooden spoon, a fork, a spoon.

What to do

Basic dip: cream cheese, yoghurt or mayonnaise.
Put the cream cheese into a mixing bowl and mash it with a fork until it is smooth and creamy, then stir in the yoghurt or mayonnaise. This makes a basic dip which can be varied by adding other ingredients.

Tuna dip
Make the basic dip but use mayonnaise rather than yoghurt. Drain the tuna and mash it up with a fork, then stir it into the dip mixture.

Chocolate truffles

What you need

Ingredients: 225g plain chocolate, three tablespoons unsweetened evaporated milk, one teaspoon vanilla essence, 115g icing sugar, chocolate vermicelli, shredded coconut.

Equipment: a mixing bowl, a saucepan, a wooden spoon, cake cases.

What to do

Break the chocolate into small pieces and melt it slowly in a bowl over a saucepan of hot water. Do not heat it too much, just to melting point. Stir in the evaporated milk, vanilla and sugar. Remove from heat and allow to cool slowly.

Sprinkle a little icing sugar on your fingers and shape the mixture into small balls. Sprinkle some of the balls with vermicelli and the rest with shredded coconut. Place in cake cases and leave to harden in a cold place. The truffles can be eaten at the Christmas party or wrapped prettily and given as presents.

Avocado dip

Cut the avocado in half and dig out the stone with a spoon. Scoop the inside into a bowl and add the juice of one lemon. Mash the avocado with a fork, add the basic mixture and mix it all together.

Let the children experiment with lots of different ingredients to make their own special party dips. They can be decorated in a variety of ways with crisps, sliced vegetables and fruit.

Butterscotch fudge

What you need

Ingredients: one cup sweetened condensed milk, two cups castor sugar, four tablespoons butter, a few drops butterscotch essence, four tablespoons water.

Equipment: a heavy-bottomed saucepan, a whisk, a buttered tray.

What to do

Cover the bottom of the saucepan with butter and place all ingredients in it. Warm over a low heat, stirring continuously until the sugar has dissolved. The following stage should be done by an adult. Bring the mixture to boil and continue boiling for ten minutes. Remove the pan from the heat and beat the mixture hard until it has thickened. This will take several minutes and is very important or the fudge will not set. Turn the mixture into a buttered tray and leave it in the refrigerator or a cool place to set. When it is ready, the children can cut it into evenly sized squares. The fudge can be packed into a presentation box to be given as a present.

Holly leaf biscuits

What you need

Ingredients: 225g self-raising flour, 1½ level teaspoons cinnamon, a pinch of salt, 150g butter, 100g castor sugar, a beaten egg.
For the icing: 225g icing sugar, a few drops of green food colouring, and, for the berries, marzipan and red food colouring.

Equipment: a sieve, a large basin, a polythene bag, a rolling pin, a greased baking tray, a round-ended knife, a pastry cutter.

What to do

Sift the flour, salt and cinnamon together in a basin, then rub in the butter until it

Set the oven at 350 degrees F or Gas Mark 4 and place the biscuits on a greased baking tray. Bake for twelve to fifteen minutes. Leave the biscuits to cool and prepare the icing.

Mix the icing sugar and water together to make a fairly stiff paste. Colour it with green food colouring and spread on the biscuits when they have cooled. Add the red food colouring to the marzipan and roll it into small berries. Press them into the moist icing and sprinkle with a little more icing sugar to give the appearance of snow.

A Christmas log

What you need

Ingredients: a packet of digestive biscuits, 1 teaspoon icing sugar, 1 teaspoon cocoa powder, 1 small pot double cream, a little extra icing sugar, holly sprigs and a plastic robin for decoration.

Equipment: a basin, a whisk, a fork, a knife, a teaspoon, a plate, aluminium foil.

What to do

Put cream, sugar and cocoa in the basin and whisk together until the mixture is stiff enough to stand up in peaks. Spread the biscuits with the mixture and then sandwich them together to make a long roll. When all the biscuits are joined together, cover the log with the rest of the mixture and run the prongs of the fork over the surface to give the appearance of tree bark. Sprinkle icing sugar over the top to look like snow and decorate with a sprig of holly and a little robin.

looks like breadcrumbs. Add the sugar and mix it all together, then add the egg and mix to a stiff dough. Knead the dough, then put it into a polythene bag and leave it in the fridge for half an hour. Roll it out to a thickness of about 1 cm and cut into holly leaf shapes using the round-ended knife or a pastry cutter.

St Nicholas' letter biscuits

What you need

Ingredients: 400g double-crust pastry, 200g marzipan, a little flour, sugar, milk.

Equipment: a greased baking sheet, a rolling pin, a round-ended knife, a pastry brush, a pastry board.

What to do

On St Nicholas' Day (6 December), Dutch children are given St Nicholas' letter biscuits to eat. This is how to make them.

Set the oven to 425 degrees F or Gas Mark 7. Sprinkle the board with flour to stop the pastry from sticking. Roll the pastry out thinly and cut into strips about 10cm × 2cm. Roll the marzipan into thin worms and sprinkle with a little sugar. Wrap the strip of pastry around the marzipan worm, dab a little milk along the edges and gently press the two edges together. Now bend each roll into the shape of a letter, taking care not to break it.

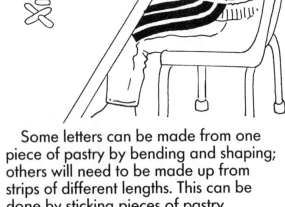

Some letters can be made from one piece of pastry by bending and shaping; others will need to be made up from strips of different lengths. This can be done by sticking pieces of pastry together, using the milk as a glue.

Carefully place the finished letters on a greased baking sheet, leaving a little space between them. Place in the centre of the oven for 10 to 15 minutes. When the biscuits are golden brown, take them out and carefully remove from the tray.

Mincemeat

What you need

Ingredients: 125g raisins, one teaspoon of mixed spice, 125g sultanas, 225g currants, 225g cooking apples, 2½ teaspoons ground ginger, 125g suet, 1 lemon, 125g mixed peel, 125g soft brown sugar, 50g chopped almonds.

Equipment: a clean tea-towel, a chopping board, a round-ended knife, a fine grater, a lemon squeezer, a sieve, a teaspoon, a large bowl, a small bowl, a wooden spoon, jam-jars, waxed-paper discs, cellophane, rubber bands.

What to do

Place the currants, raisins and sultanas in the sieve and wash them under the cold tap. Shake them well, then tip them on to the tea-towel and pat them to remove any excess water. Tip them into the large bowl and add the almonds, mixed peel, spices, sugar and suet. Peel the apples, cut them into quarters and remove the core. Put the apples on the chopping board and chop them up into small pieces. Add them to the dried fruit mixture.

Now wash and dry the lemon. Using the fine grater, gently grate the zest into the small bowl. Cut the lemon in half and squeeze out all the juice. Add the juice and the grated peel to the large bowl and mix it well using the wooden spoon. Leave this mixture covered for twenty-four hours.

Sterilise some jam-jars so that the mincemeat can be spooned in. You can buy sterilising solution from the chemists. Spoon the mincemeat into the sterilised jam-jars. Place a waxed disc on top of the mincemeat and cover either with a screw-top or with a cellophane circle held in place with a rubber band. The mincemeat will be best if it is left for at least two weeks before using.

Chocolate apples

What you need

Ingredients: eating apples, lollipop sticks, unsweetened cooking chocolate, chocolate vermicelli or hundreds and thousands.

Equipment: a saucepan half-filled with boiling water, a heatproof basin, a wooden spoon, waxed paper, absorbent paper.

What to do

First of all, wash the apples and dry on a sheet of absorbent paper. Push a lollipop stick firmly into each apple at the point where the stalk sticks out. Break the cooking chocolate into small pieces and put into the heatproof basin. Place it on top of a pan of gently simmering water. When the chocolate is soft and runny, remove the basin from the saucepan and dip each apple in chocolate. Make sure the apple is well covered by turning it around in the chocolate. Lift the apple out carefully and roll it in the vermicelli or the hundreds and thousands. Stand the apples with the sticks pointing upwards on the waxed paper and leave them in a cold place or a refrigerator to set.

Variation: Chocolate cherries can be prepared in the same way, using glace cherries and cocktail sticks. They make a delicious addition to the Christmas party.

Puppets and scenery

Chapter ten

Puppets are a fascinating extension of the hand and the self for all age groups. This chapter offers some very simple ideas for making puppets with different materials, involving different handling techniques suitable for this age group. We have also included some ideas for puppet theatres, as the mini-world of the puppet is just as interesting to the small child.

A walking snowman

What you need
White card, silver glitter, assorted colours of felt, scissors, felt-tipped pens, adhesive.

What to do
Draw and cut a snowman shape out of white card, making it about 12cm in height. An adult will need to cut the finger holes, about 2cm from the bottom and 2cm apart.

The snowman can now be decorated with a face and buttons drawn with felt-tipped pens, and a hat and scarf cut from felt. Those children advanced enough in hand control may be able to cut their own if help is given with the sizes.

The puppet is operated as shown in the illustration. Variations on this theme include a clown, Father Christmas, a fairy or any pantomime characters.

Instead of drawing figures, you can use cut-out figures from Christmas cards.

Waving puppets

What you need
Fabric, a green garden stick, materials needed for 'A calendar man' (see page 46), scissors, adhesive, sticky tape.

What to do
Make a model figure as for 'A calendar man' but, instead of the paper arms, use a strip of fabric such as felt and make it long enough to wiggle if you hold the loose end. If you use another fabric, stick a felt hand on the end.

Tape or glue a garden stick to the back of one hand and the puppet is complete. To operate it, put one hand inside the body and hold the stick with your other hand to wave, gesticulate and generally help the 'act'.

The Nativity with straw puppets

What you need

Old greetings cards, white card, art straws or plastic straws, glitter, felt-tipped pens, scissors, sticky tape, adhesive.

What to do

Cut out or draw all the characters for the Nativity story. Several children can work together to do this. Leave a lip of card at the bottom of the figure and fold it to the back. Add glitter where appropriate.

Using sticky tape, fix the end of a straw to the inside of the fold of card. Hold the straw to move the figure on the set.

The Nativity set

What you need

An old shoe-box, a small box, a cut-out picture of a baby, paint, art straws, paintbrushes, adhesive, scissors.

What to do

Paint the shoe-box inside and out, using a mixture of greys, yellows and browns to represent stone or wood. If you decide on wood, paint the walls in vertical stripes; if stone, dab the paint on and merge the colours. The artists may want to paint the floor yellow to represent straw.

To do the roof, cut the straws to the appropriate length, lay them on a bed of glue and when dry, paint yellow for straw or brown for logs.

A manger can be made from a small box painted brown. Add a few straws cut vertically to make finer straw and a cut-out picture of the baby Jesus.

The straw puppets can be operated in front of and inside the stable set.

A puppet theatre

What you need

A medium-sized cardboard box, paint in assorted colours, red or blue crêpe paper, glitter, gold foil, parcel ribbon, white card, adhesive, a stapler, scissors, sticky tape, felt-tipped pens, bottle tops.

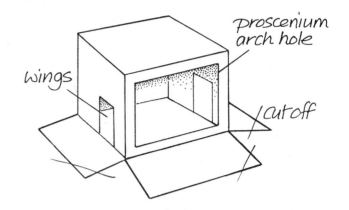

What to do

Trim the box as shown in the illustration. Cut a large rectangular hole in one side for the proscenium arch and a small rectangle at each side for the wings.

Paint the outside of the box in a colour that tones well with the colour of crêpe paper you have decided to use. Then paint the inside in a very light colour to reflect light near the characters.

To make the curtains, cut two pieces of crêpe paper about 25cm wide and as deep as the box. Gather each piece at the top and staple to make a gather of about 6cm, then glue this to the top of each side of the arch. You can decorate the top of the arch by sticking gold foil to one of the longest discarded flaps. This can be cut as in the illustration and glued to the top front to hide the curtain gathers and the cut edge of the box. The footlights are made by covering the front edge of the box with a strip of gold foil and then adding bottle tops on the inside for the lights.

To complete the theatre, ties can be added to the curtains with wool or parcel ribbon. Different backdrops can be made using sheets of white paper or card, with felt-tipped pen artwork secured in place with small rolls of sticky tape.

The theatre can be used on a table top, with the straw puppets pushed into view through the wings, or if it is placed over the edge of the table, glove puppets can be used moving upwards.

Felt finger puppets

What you need

Assorted felt, sequins, scraps of coloured paper and wool, Copydex adhesive, scissors.

To assemble the puppet, paint a thin line of adhesive all round the sides and the top curve, leaving the bottom edge open and press the other finger on top. You need very small amounts of adhesive to secure the pieces and even the youngest children can work carefully at this. Glue the face on and stick sequins on for eyes and scraps of felt for the mouth. Triangular hats, crowns, hair, buttons and bows can be added. Let the adhesive dry overnight before trying out the puppets.

The youngest children can put two fingers inside the puppet and may find it easier to use it this way.

Push-along puppets

What you need

White card, felt-tipped pens or crayons, scissors, a paper fastener, thick straw, sticky tape.

What to do

Using the card, cut out a figure as shown, about 15cm long, and a circle about 8cm in diameter. The artist can then draw in details to make the character he or she wants. It could be Father Christmas, a funny animal or a clown. The legs of the character are to be drawn on the circle and most children will need to be carefully shown where and how to draw them (see illustration).

To assemble the puppet, put the leg circle behind the figure so that one leg is showing in the correct forward position. Make a hole through the two pieces about 1cm from the bottom of the figure. An adult should do this. The child can then push the paper fastener through the two and open it out.

Tape a short piece of card for a handle to the back of the figure and push it along the table.

What to do

Cut two fingers of felt 5cm × 8cm and curve it at the top. Cut a circle of felt for the face and an assortment of triangles, bow shapes, circles and strips which can be used to decorate the puppets.

Scenery

The following are a few suggestions for how the children can contribute to the scenery for Christmas productions.

Trees, bushes and walls

What you need

Large rolls of corrugated card, assorted paint, assorted sponge shapes, sponge washing-up mops, 1cm paintbrushes, flat containers for paint, scissors, a stapler.

What to do

Cut the card to the size and shape you require. Lay it flat, with the smooth side uppermost, on spread-out newspaper for painting.

Different effects can be achieved with sponges and even the youngest children can use this technique. The paint containers need to be shallow and you may need to top up supplies, so have extra paint in reserve. Rectangular sponges can be used for a stone-wall effect and can be cut into leaf shapes for shrubbery and trees. A sponge washing-up mop made of strips of sponge on a plastic handle is very useful for leaves and desert sands.

The technique with sponge is to dip it into the paint and wipe off the excess, then press the sponge firmly on to the paper, reloading when the paint gets faint. A variation in depth of colour gives a depth to the picture so do not worry about perfect prints. With the washing-up mop, just dip in and dab on! Use two or even three shades of the same colour to add interest to the wall or the tree and, for the latter, add some painted leaf shapes with a sharp outline.

Let the corrugated card dry thoroughly on a flat surface before moving. When dry, fix it into position with a stapler. Wings such as these can be stapled or taped to the edge of walls or round the edge of stage blocks. Cardboard centres from rolls of carpet are also useful for such anchor points and can often be obtained from carpet showrooms.

Backdrops and buildings

What you need

Materials as above.

What to do

The backdrop: Large sheets of paper can sometimes be obtained from manufacturers and billboard printers and these are ideal for backdrops. They can be stapled in position for painting or laid flat on the floor. Failing that, old bed sheets can be used. To hang these, you will need two lengths of wood, to which the sheet can be stapled. This frame can then be hung in position on hooks.

To paint the scene, use sponges, either to print with or to wipe on the paint. Simple scenes are most effective, for example:
- A night sky – dark blue wiped all over, left to dry, and grey clouds sponge-printed with rough shapes. Gold-foil stars can be cut out and stuck on.
- A stable – sponge-printed stone wall with a space for a small window. Print a row of stone blocks round this and fill the space with dark blue and a single large silver-foil star.
- Woodland – three or four large tree shapes sponge-printed with different shapes of leaves in assorted shades of green paint. Greyish-brown trunks can be added and the sponge mop or a large emulsion brush used to dab on a grassy mound at the baseline.

Buildings: Fit corrugated card round large items of furniture such as a piano, a PE mat stand, a 'horse' or a cupboard, and then lay flat for painting.

Using sponges and a variety of shades of paint, fill the card with stone blocks, marking out a window and a door (see illustration). Fill in the window hole with yellow for light and the door with smooth lines for wood effect. When they are dry, tape or staple to the mount.

Index of materials

Items are classified according to the main material used to achieve the finished effect.

Paper

Stripy shapes 11
A big bauble 10
Snowflake hangings 10
Decorated fir trees 14
Stained-glass windows 16
Snow fans 23
A Christmas tree 28
Table Christmas tree 29
A Christmas cracker place-mat 30
An everlasting calendar 48
A paper sculpture calendar 49
A collage calendar 50
Simple hats 69
Crepe skirts and cloaks 70
A winter evening 74
A stocking full of wishes 74

Plastics

Window decorations 13
Fairies for the tree-top 20
A tree cracker 21
A candle table centre 29
A jewelled tree 36
A bauble card 38
A sequin tree card 39
A stained-glass window 51
Bouncing bits 52
A royal crown 66
The evening star 66

Glues

A candle hanger 14
A glitter drawing 36
A starry night 37
Glitzy wrapping-paper 41

Cardboard

A chimney-pot post-box 12

A candle on each branch 22
Doves of peace 23
A Christmas cracker napkin ring 30
A party place-name 31
A party hat cutlery holder 31
A family bus trip 44
Our house 44
A self-portrait in a gilt frame 45
A calendar man 46
A desk tidy 56
A golden halo 64
A starship circlet 64
A robin in the evergreens 65
Animals and birds 67
A party-time mask 67
A second face 68
A knight of the realm 70
A 3-D snow scene 77
The Nativity set 91
A puppet theatre 92
Push-along puppets 93
Scenery 94

Natural materials

Glitter-and-seed mobiles 11
An oak-leaf decoration 24
A painted pine-cone 25
A pine-cone Christmas tree 28
A green greeting 38
A fern tree 39
A pomander 54
A jewelled paperweight 55
A vase of dried flowers 58
A wall hanging 61

Fabric

Fairy folk 18
Bookmark 56
A decorated box 58
Bookends 59
A Christmas pudding tea-cosy 60
Decorating fabric 72
Three fancy kins 76
Waving puppets 90

Felt finger puppets 92

Clay

A candle holder 32
Clay holly leaves 34

Paint

Dribbled Christmas stockings 15
Marbled candles 32
A print of Rudolf 36
When Santa got stuck up the chimney 40
Dazzlingly bright wrapping-paper 41
Marbled wrapping-paper 42
A monoprint masterpiece 46
A decorated notebook 57
A Nativity scene 75
A thumb-print picture 76
A Christmas painting 78

Glass

Christmas lanterns 33
A snowstorm 54

Metals

A wall frieze 12
A Christmas rose 18
An antique metal plaque 50

Wood

A dog-lead holder 58
A key tidy 62

Food

Pasta garlands 19
Spaghetti stars 24
Pasta baubles 26
A pasta card 38
Pasta necklaces 60
Cookery Chapter 9 79